LORD, I

WISH MY HUSBAND WOULD PRAY WITH ME

LORD, I WISH MY HUSBAND WOULD PRAY WITH ME

LARRY KEEFAUVER, D. MIN.

CREATION HOUSE
Orlando, FL

LORD, I WISH MY HUSBAND WOULD PRAY WITH ME
by Larry Keefauver, D.Min.
Published by Creation House
Strang Communications Company
600 Rinehart Road
Lake Mary, Florida 32746
Web site: http://www.creationhouse.com

Unless otherwise noted, all Scripture quotations are from the Holy Bible, New International Version. Copyright © 1973, 1978, 1984, International Bible Society. Used by permission.

Scripture quotations marked KJV are from the King James Version of the Bible.

Scripture quotations marked NAS are from the New American Standard Bible. Copyright © 1960, 1962, 1963, 1968, 1971, 1972, 1973, 1975, 1977 by the Lockman Foundation. Used by permission.

Scripture quotations marked NLT are from the Holy Bible, New Living Translation, copyright © 1996. Used by permission of Tyndale House Publishers, Inc., Wheaton, IL 60189. All rights reserved.

Library of Congress Cataloging-in-Publication data:
Keefauver, Larry.
    Lord, I wish my husband would pray with me / Larry Keefauver,
        p.   c.m.   Includes bibliographical references.
    ISBN: 0-88419-528-7 (pbk.)
    1. Wives—Religious life. 2. Wives—Prayer-books and devotions—
English.
I. Title.
BV4527.K44 1998   97-48933
284.8'435—dc21   CIP

Historical prayers used at the beginning of chapters are adapted from *Prayers Across the Centuries*, edited by Vinita Hampton (Wheaton, IL: Harold Shaw Publishers, 1993).

Printed in the United States of America
89012345 BBG 87654321

Dedicated to my supportive and praying wife,
Judi,
who prayed for me
long before we ever prayed together.

I thank Jesus for Judi!

Acknowledgments

I praise the Lord and want to thank those
who diligently helped with and guided this book—

Tom Freiling, my publisher and friend;

the editorial team at Creation House:
Alyse Lounsberry, Barbara Dycus,
Lillian McAnally, Debbie Moss, and Karen Judge;

Steve and Joy Strang;

and the women's groups who reviewed
the manuscript and gave such insightful input.

Contents

Introduction..*xi*

1 Are You Asleep, or Are You Praying? 1

2 If You Aren't the Priest of the Family,
   Who Is? 11

BREAKING DOWN THE SPIRITUAL WALLS OF ...

3 Unfulfilled Expectations, Unimplemented Plans,
   and Unkept Promises 37

4 Unmet Needs, Unprized Gifts,
   and Unrecognized Sacrifices..69

5 Unhealed Hurts, Unresolved Anger,
   and Unrepented Offenses...99

6 Unconfessed Sin, Undignified Communication,
   and Unfeeling Responses 123

7 Confession:
   Repentance That Heals Marriages................................155

8 A Final Prayer 179

Notes *189*

Appendix: Praying From the Scriptures........................*191*

Select Bibliography...*209*

Help me, Lord, to remember that religion is not to be confined to the church or closet, nor exercised only in prayer and meditation, but that everywhere I am in your presence. So may my every word and action have moral content.

—Susanna Wesley
17th–18th Century a.d.

INTRODUCTION

For more than twenty-five years I have been a pastoral counselor, teacher, and pastor. Literally thousands of counseling sessions with married couples have revealed to me some of the unfulfilled spiritual needs in the lives of husbands and wives. More often than their husbands, wives express their needs for spiritual intimacy, prayer, learning God's Word, and sharing the deep things of God with their husbands. For the hundreds of times I heard wives sigh, "I wish my husband would pray with me," I rarely hear any husband express that desire. Why?

Are wives more spiritually sensitive than husbands? Do they discern spiritual lack before their husbands? What bricks have been laid in the spiritual wall that is built between husbands and wives? As a husband I have found myself praying more as a pastor and counselor with others than with my wife. Consequently, I have tried gimmicks, felt guilty, withdrawn, bought books, sought spiritual counsel, and even argued with my wife and others over what should happen spiritually between Christian spouses. So we have personally struggled with all of these issues and have learned from God's Word, His Spirit, the wise counsel of others, and from practical experience how to share spiritually.

This book has been written for wives. I am writing to wives from a male perspective for the purpose of imparting understanding—not condemnation, commands, and criticism. Statistics reveal that husbands go to Christian bookstores and buy books less frequently than their wives—much less books on marriage and spirituality! Reality is that wives almost always discern a spiritual wall in a marriage before their husbands and are willing to face it and dismantle it well before their husbands will ever admit to any problem. So, precious wife, here are some insights into what's happening, how to understand it, ways to pray about it, and yes, some very practical helps for actually growing with your husband in prayer and spiritual disciplines.

And since your husband may never willingly read this book—even if you leave it opened under his channel controller or on his pillow with underlined paragraphs highlighted for his attention—try reading it aloud to him before sex or before allowing the silver mesmerizer called TV to be turned on to ESPN, CNNSI, or the latest cable sports package that he so eagerly wants to watch.

Actually, praying with him before the big game involving his favorite team could be much more productive than trying to pray just after his team has lost the big one! I would wish you luck, but luck has nothing to do with what you desire. I am wishing you godly perseverance. Your desire to pray and share spiritually with your husband isn't just your idea—it's God's idea—and it will reap eternal benefits. Forge ahead with boldness. Judi and I are praying together for you!

Give us, O Lord, steadfast hearts that cannot be dragged down by false loves; give us courageous hearts that cannot be worn down by trouble; give us righteous hearts that cannot be sidetracked by unholy or unworthy goals. Give to us also, our Lord and God, understanding to know You, diligence to look for You, wisdom to recognize You, and a faithfulness that will bring us to see You face to face.

—THOMAS À KEMPIS
14TH–15TH CENTURY A.D.

1

ARE YOU ASLEEP, OR ARE YOU PRAYING?

THAT PARTICULAR NIGHT started off no different than any other. My wife, Judi, and I had gone to bed, watched some late night news, read our respective devotionals, and turned the lights off after kissing one another good night. As the darkness enfolded us and fuzzy clouds of semiconsciousness drifted into my brain, I concluded my day as I always had since childhood—by praying.

For years I had prayed myself to sleep. Starting with my wife and children, I would pray for all those that came to mind and rehearse both their needs and my praise for them until finally the curtains closed, my thoughts drifted, and sleep enveloped me until daybreak.

Morning followed a similar pattern. After the alarm sounded two or three times, my thoughts would once again focus on the Lord—thanking Him for the new day while praying protection and blessing upon my family and my upcoming hectic schedule.

Yet on that particular night, right before I drifted into oblivion, a piercing light penetrated my closed eyelids and my wife's voice jarred me before the Almighty's judgment seat:

"Well...are you asleep...or are you praying?"

Immediately adrenaline jolted my brain, and holier-than-thou tones shaped my vocal cords.

"Praying, of course," I intoned.

"How can you be so hypocritical?" she asked accusingly.

"What in the world...," I offered, only to be abruptly interrupted like a derailed freight train.

"There you stand in the pulpit every week extolling the virtues of prayer, and you don't even pray with your wife!" she accused—quite accurately, I must admit.

"But I do pray for you, and for the children, and for..."

"That's not what I mean...and don't try to defend yourself. You're a self-righteous...," she shouted as both of us now sat up and prepared for the next sequel to *Rocky*.

"What brought this on?" I asked.

"You would think...," she proceeded, like a criminal trial prosecutor who knows that the defendant is nakedly guilty with no mitigating circumstances. "You would think that at least once a week or so you would stoop so low as to pray with your wife—since you make it a point to pray publicly with elders, deacons, church members, and even strangers. I'm just asking for equal time, you hypocrite!"

That first flurry of righteous jabs and dogmatic left hooks happened just a few years after I had entered the full-time ministry as a youth pastor. The truth is, after twenty-five years of pastoring, counseling, teaching, and writing, I still fail to live up to all of Judi's expectations (and mine!) concerning my prayer and spiritual life. Thank God she's not on His judgment seat at the end of time!

However, we are still married—happily and joyfully. We often pray together both aloud and silently. And we still disagree about some issues in the church. I am still pastoring, teaching, and writing, and she is still a living reminder of the many ways I fall short of spiritually being all that God has created me to be. Then again, all of us fall short (Rom. 3:23). Thank God for grace!

So what prompted this book about the spiritual crises that wives and husbands face as Christians? What can be said that hasn't already been written in the scores of books about Christian marriages, couples' devotional times, and the endless parade of videos, tapes, and study guides focusing on marital spirituality?

Simply this: Too many husbands and fathers struggle constantly with false guilt and condemnation about their failure to be the spiritual giants their wives, families, and churches preach that they should be. Oh, you've heard all the lofty ideals:

> The father is the high priest of the family.
> Men need to take their rightful places as spiritual heads of their families and marriages.
> If men in the church were as spiritual as the women, more ministry would happen; deeper prayers would be prayed; and revival would break out in the church.

3

❯ Women are tired of being the spiritual leaders of the home. It's time that the men stepped up to the plate and started swinging at the flying missiles Satan is hurling at the family.

❯ What we need today are more men like we read about in the Bible—spiritual giants like Abraham, Samuel, and David. (If the truth be known, many of the men of God in the Bible failed greatly at being good husbands and fathers.)

Hold on! This book is not a defense of spiritually inept, lazy, biblically illiterate, materialistic men who neglect or abuse their families and who fail to take their faith seriously. But this is a book for husbands and wives who are tired of feeling like spiritual failures or nags and desire to get on with growing together in Christ.

It's time to set aside the polemics and the unrealistic expectations as well as the accusations, condemnations, and guilt trips. Spiritual crises in marriages and families can either build faith or become wrecking balls that destroy fragile spiritual foundations and crush any hope of growing together in Christ.

Christian couples face tremendous spiritual challenges. But they are not without biblical wisdom and wonderful examples from other believers in how to grow through these crises without pulling up and dropping out of the race toward the finish line (Heb. 12:1–3). It's time for Christian marriages not just to survive spiritually—but to finish strong!

After many years of marriage counseling, pastoring, and sharing with fellow Christian couples on similar journeys of faith, we have not only identified some of the common crises, but we have also seen some God-given means of grace available to help couples grow together—not apart—in Christ.

DO YOU FIND YOURSELF ASKING . . .

▶ How can we pray together so that both of us are comfortable, real, transparent, and honest?

▶ When one feels more spiritual than the other, what do we do?

▶ What has caused the spiritual wall between us, and how can it be torn down?

▶ When life is falling apart at home, why go to church and feel worse, guilty, or hypocritical?

▶ What should we do when we are too busy *doing* church work to *be* the church in worship and ministry?

▶ How do we stop arguing about tithing and finances?

▶ Which church is right for us?

▶ How do we change churches without hurting others or being hurt?

▶ When family devotions aren't working for us, should we give up?

▶ Where is the balance between Christian television and other channels—between Christian music and other types of music?

▶ Both of us are so busy and tired that we don't have any time together, much less time to pray and read Scripture together—so what now?

▶ Our kids want to go to another church, and we love it right where we are—should we make them stay with us?

▶ We can't agree on what we believe, where to

5

worship, or how to raise our children spiritually—who's right?

> How do I minister to my husband or wife when he or she is in a personal, spiritual crisis?

Let me assure you that these crises are real. Like a deadly twister on a stormy day, a spiritual crisis can overtake anyone. Pastors' families as well as church members' families can face a spiritual crisis at any time. Spiritual crises are watershed events in our lives that build walls of separation—or that break them down.

SPIRITUAL CRISES ARE . . .

WHAT IS A spiritual crisis in a marriage or a family? A spiritual crisis is . . .

> A moment when spouses are tempted to move *apart* instead of *together* in Christ.
> A word or action that spiritually wounds a marriage.
> A decision that must be made that hangs in the balance between absolute truth and compromising relativism.
> An offense, conflict, or strife that tempts one (or both) spouse to be unforgiving toward the other.

A spiritual crisis can be complex—such as one spouse who trusts Jesus and the other spouse who lives in unbelief—or simple—such as disagreements over whether or not to go to church on a particular Sunday morning.

One wife, who constantly nagged her husband

about spiritual matters, was having a tough time getting him up and ready for church. "I am not your mother," she protested to him. "I'm tired of having to force you to get up and go to church with me every Sunday morning. What's wrong with you?"

"But the people there hate me," her husband answered.

"No, they don't," she fired back.

"And the service is boring," he retorted.

"You should be worshiping God, not analyzing the service," she instructed.

"And they are always fighting and bickering," he complained. "I would be better off staying home than listening to that!"

"But you have to go!" his wife insisted.

"Why?" he demanded.

"Because you're the preacher!" she exclaimed.

Yes, it's an old story. But the lesson remains timeless. No matter how dedicated, committed, educated, spiritual, or devoted a couple is to Christ and His church, there will be times of spiritual crisis. Clergy couples are no more immunized to spiritual crises than the couples in the pew. So we do not have to wonder which segment of the church is affected by prayerlessness—every person and every marriage will, at one time or another, face spiritual crises that may build walls of prayerlessness between husbands and wives.

THE CRITICAL QUESTION

WILL SPIRITUAL CRISIS be a time of *constructing walls* or of *breaking down* spiritual walls as a couple?

Each upcoming chapter will:

7

▶ Define spiritual barriers commonly faced by Christian couples in their marriages and church life.

▶ Defuse the issue by refusing to project full blame on either person, seeking rather to be quick to listen, slow to speak, and slow to anger while sharing the truth in love.

▶ Help wives to understand what's going on in their husbands' spiritual lives.

▶ Reveal biblical wisdom about the spiritual walls from God's perspective—not ours.

▶ Uncover new and fresh ways to break down spiritual walls and discover deeper intimacy in Christ.

▶ Challenge you to try new attitudes and behaviors that will see you through your spiritual barriers and make your marriage an example for others in the body of Christ.

Still there? Are you asleep, or are you praying?

••

BY THE WAY, THOSE WHO THINK THEY NEED THIS BOOK THE LEAST PROBABLY NEED IT THE MOST! ARE YOU READY TO LEARN HOW TO FINISH STRONG AFTER FACING A SPIRITUAL CRISIS? THEN TURN THE PAGE AND LET'S GET STARTED BREAKING DOWN THE SPIRITUAL WALLS BETWEEN YOU AND YOUR HUSBAND.

••

Lord,

You know that we need You and each other. Grant us the desire to grow deeper and closer to You through praying together. Make us sensitive to every spiritual barrier between us. Help us to be bold and committed as we dismantle each spiritual wall separating us from one another and You.

And finally, Lord, even when pulling down walls is painful, strengthen us with patience and perseverance so that we may pray together in power and agreement.
In Jesus' name.

—Amen

Forgive them all, O Lord…

Our sins of omission and our sins of commission;
The sins of our youth and the sins of our riper years;
The sins of our souls and the sins of our bodies;
Our secret and our more open sins;
Our sins of ignorance and surprise, and our more deliberate and presumptuous sins;
The sins we have done to please ourselves and the sins we have done to please others;
The sins we know and remember, and the sins we have forgotten;
The sins we have striven to hide from others and the sins by which we have made others offend;
Forgive them, O Lord, forgive them all for His sake who died for our sins and rose for our justification, and now stands at Your right hand to make intercession for us, Jesus Christ our Lord.

—JOHN WESLEY
18TH CENTURY A.D.

2

IF YOU AREN'T THE PRIEST
OF THE FAMILY, WHO IS?

OUR HOME GROUP had started innocently enough.
Everyone shared prayer requests, and then the
leader suggested we all hold hands and pray aloud.
The leader's wife would start the prayer time, and
everyone in the circle would have the opportunity to
pray (whether they wanted it or not!). The circle of
prayer would progress clockwise with each person
interceding as he or she was led by the Holy Spirit.

The problem was that Steve only did "closet"
praying—never "circle" praying. Never before had
he prayed in public. In fact, this was the first home
group he had ever attended.

For weeks prior to this night Jennifer had worked
Steve over like a boxer pounding at his opponent's
midriff until finally Steve had folded over and given
up to her ten-count. Much to his dismay he found
himself in a church home group.

Yes, everything he had feared about such groups

had happened. First, Steve was asked to share about himself in front of the whole group. He hated talking in front of groups of more than two unless it happened to be about football or coaching soccer. Next, the group leader had paired Steve with an extroverted lawyer with whom he was to share his feelings about forgiveness. The lawyer grilled Steve while never divulging a thing about himself.

Then everyone had to share a prayer need or a praise report. He couldn't think of a need he could share. (He'd never let this group know how terrified he was of his daughter's approaching sixteenth birthday and her desire to date.) Since Steve couldn't share about his real fears, he made something up that sounded pious and spiritual.

Now this moment for prayer came. For what seemed like hours, he stood holding hands with near strangers. (Jennifer was on the other side of the circle with her partner.) Steve always sweated when he held hands. He never held hands with Jennifer because sweaty palms embarrassed him. Now, both sweating and thoroughly embarrassed, he was holding hands with two men he had just met.

A spiritual crisis overtook him like a mad junkyard dog chasing the trash collector. Waves of nausea washed over him—it was his time to pray in public!

Jim, the guy next to Steve, had just completed the world's longest prayer for the lost of the sub-division, town, state, nation, and world. Now it was Steve's turn to pray.

Barely mumbling above a whisper, Steve stammered, "Thank You, God, for my wife and family. Amen."

If the home group hadn't been bad enough, the

ride home with Jennifer was worse.

"You embarrassed me so much tonight I don't know if we can ever show our faces at church again," she blurted out as soon as they backed out of the driveway.

"But you know how I hate to pray out loud, especially in a public place," Steve shot back defensively. "Don't worry about going back to face those folks. The next time I'll see them will be in heaven—if I make it!"

"That's exactly what I mean about you. You have no spiritual backbone. No leadership in our family. Didn't you hear a word that Pastor preached Sunday?" she asked.

Steve gripped the steering wheel so tightly that his knuckles began to turn white. Canyons formed in his forehead as anger bubbled like a volcano and fomented right beneath his forced, calm exterior. This argument played out like a repeat video that always had the same ending—the silent treatment from Jennifer for a few days.

"I heard every word," Steve forced through clenched jaws.

"Well, just to remind you, Pastor clearly taught that you are the priest of the family. I'm tired of having to take the lead on every spiritual issue in our marriage from prayer to reading the Bible, getting the kids ready for church, getting you to go to a home group where we could make some Christian friends and have a little fellowship. If you had your way, we would sit at home in front of the television watching sports every night of the week!"

Seizing the opportunity and hoping to put his wife on the defensive, Steve quickly replied, "Now

13

Saint Jennie, isn't that language a little strong for Joan of Arc?" The moment he said it Steve knew he had once again crossed the line. She folded her arms, glared straight ahead, and began a total fast of words that would last for several weeks. The war of silence had once again commenced. Tragically, the fight was over spiritual things—like prayer and the Bible—which were supposed to bring peace, love, power, and closeness into a marriage. What had gone wrong? Could the spiritual crisis be resolved and even avoided the next time—if there was a next time?

SPIRITUAL CRISIS #1—WHO'S THE PRIEST OR SPIRITUAL LEADER IN THE FAMILY?

PRIEST ZECHARIAH PRAYED. Elizabeth had faith. Together they were awesome vessels used of God to prepare the way for the Messiah (Luke 1).

Both these spouses exercised their spiritual gifts, and God responded to their need. A Levite by birth, not necessarily by disposition, Zechariah served God faithfully in the temple during the time of King Herod. Elizabeth had been childless for years. It is the heart cry of every Jewish husband to father children and to pass on his family name and seed to subsequent generations. Offspring were so important that the Torah provided for a man's brother to marry his widow and birth a son to carry on the name of his deceased father. (See Deuteronomy 25:5–6.) This was the basis of the marriage between Boaz and Ruth.

Zechariah had observed the Law blamelessly and prayed for a son (Luke 1:5–17). Yet when an angel from the Lord revealed that childless Elizabeth would have a son, Zechariah had a lapse of faith and questioned God, "How can I be sure of this? I am an old man and my wife is well along in years" (Luke 1:18). Does this sound like the words of a strong, spiritual leader in his family? Not hardly. Zechariah's lack of faith caused him to be struck dumb, unable to speak until his son, John (the Baptist), was born. Yet when naming the baby became an issue, Elizabeth received the revelation of John's name, and Zechariah stood obediently firm in backing up her prophetic anointing: "Then they made signs to his father [Zechariah], to find out what he would like to name the child. He asked for a writing tablet, and to everyone's astonishment, he wrote, 'His name is John.' Immediately his mouth was opened and his tongue was loosed, and he began to speak, praising God" (Luke 1:62–64).

On the other hand, Elizabeth demonstrated great faith, praising God for what He had done: "The Lord has done this for me...In these days he has shown his favor and taken away my disgrace among the people" (Luke 1:25). While Zechariah's spirituality is never again mentioned, Luke reports that Elizabeth was filled with the Holy Spirit and pronounces a blessing over the coming Messiah who is within her cousin Mary's womb. (See Luke 1:39–46.)

Who's the priest in this family? Zechariah may hold the office, but Elizabeth also possessed the Holy Spirit's anointing. While Zechariah appeared to have an anointing for prayer and obedience, his wife was anointed with faith and prophetic praise and revelation. (See Luke 1.) From their example we can observe some spiritual truths:

15

➤ In a priestly family, the Spirit's anointing may rest on husband or wife.

➤ God honors and responds to the faithful initiative and obedience of *both* husband and wife.

➤ God cares more about the attitude of servanthood than the position or role one possesses.

Notice that Scripture records, "Both of them were upright in the sight of God, observing all the Lord's commandments and regulations blamelessly" (Luke 1:6).

Luke later reports in Luke 2 that another couple closely worked together spiritually to be mightily used of God—Joseph and Mary. In fact, Mary heard from God before Joseph (Luke 1:26–38; Matt. 1:18), and Joseph appears to be slightly slow on the spiritual draw—so much so that an angel comes to him personally to spell out his responsibilities (Matt. 1:19–25).

These stories suggest that both couples provide for us wonderful examples of how husbands and wives can move through spiritual crises together with either one or the other taking the spiritual initiative as the Spirit leads. The essential factor for the anointing to empower a husband or wife is not office or role but rather faithful surrender.

The truth is, marriage does not alter one of God's absolute ways of working in our midst. He uses servants. The attitude God desires in marriage is not one of rightful responsibility or powerful position. He requires of all of us that "the greatest among you will be your servant" (Matt. 23:11). Marriage does not alter or change this inviolate principle of relationships. Marriage should embody servanthood.

Paul writes that the attitude in marriage is like the church's relationship to Christ: "And further, you will submit to one another out of reverence for Christ" (Eph. 5:21, NLT).

So if you are a husband and are seeking your proper role in marriage, your first desire will be to serve your wife. As head of the wife as Christ is head of the church, one of a husband's servant acts is the act of loving his wife and laying down his life for her as Christ did for the church. The husband is a servant leader in the home. Likewise, the wife's first priority is to serve her husband.

So who is the leader in the home? The husband is.

How does he lead? Through love and service.

What does that leadership require of him? Reverence for Christ and prayer.

Why does he pray? Because as Christ prayed for the church, so he prays for his wife. (See John 17.)

Who is the priest of the home? Actually, both the husband and the wife are priests in the home. Peter writes about all Christians: "But you are a chosen people, a royal priesthood, a holy nation, a people belonging to God, that you may declare the praises of him who called you out of darkness into his wonderful light" (1 Pet. 2:9).

The only people God uses are broken people—humble servants—who are willing to be poured out in love for others. Prayer in marriage is the privilege and responsibility of both husband and wife. Christ is the High Priest of every marriage. He is the only one in the New Testament ever referred to as the High Priest. (See Hebrews 4:14–16.)

After church one Sunday morning a wife, with her husband at her side, said to me, "I've always heard that the husband is the high priest of the home. Since Jesus is head of the church, and, like Jesus, the husband is head of the home, then my husband should be the high priest in our home, and he isn't doing his job! Will you set him straight about this?" Talk about being put on the spot!

Her statement and question were more about relationship than theology. I could have exegeted some texts and quoted some experts like Gary Smalley or James Dobson. But what she really was asking for (and needed) was a husband who would pray, be a servant leader, and set an example of Christ in the home. Let's explore how a husband can fulfill the needs of a wife in the area of prayer and spiritual leadership without being forced to conform to a perceived role that she—not God— expects him to fill.

THE PRIVATE PRAYERS OF A HUSBAND

E. M. BOUNDS in his book, *Purpose in Prayer,* stated:

> Praying women and children are invaluable to God, but if their praying is not supplemented by praying men, there will be a great loss in the power of prayer, a great breach and depreciation in the value of prayer, and great paralysis in the energy of the gospel.[1]

Priests prayed and interceded for God's people in the Old Testament. (See Leviticus 9, 16, 21–22.) Christ prayed for His church in the New Testament. (See John 17.) As priests following the example of Christ, husbands pray for their wives just as Christ prayed for His bride—the church. (See Ephesians 5.)

A primary occasion of prayer for husbands is in private. I have met so many wives who fail to understand praying men at this point. Notice that I am not excluding public praying, but I am first describing private prayers.

One frustrated wife accusingly berated her husband in a Sunday school class by saying, "My husband is always praying, but never with me! Every morning he goes off by himself and prays. I just don't understand why he must always be alone to pray."

After counseling and sharing with scores of men about their prayer lives, I have discovered a reality about men praying that can also be seen in Scripture: Men have private prayer lives. Here are some of the comments they make about praying:

▶ I love praying in private but feel uncomfortable praying in public.
▶ When I pray aloud with my wife I feel like she's listening to me and critiquing what I pray.
▶ Prayer is more authentic and genuine for me when I pray alone.
▶ I become very intimate in my conversations with the Lord. It's hard for me to share that intimacy with anyone else, even my wife.
▶ My prayer relationship with the Lord is personal and private. I need time alone with Him.

Before public prayer becomes authentic, private prayer must be practiced. The practice of the presence of God begins in the privacy of a one-to-one relationship with God and then moves into a corporate, public setting of two or more people.

19

The fact that a husband may not feel comfortable praying publicly with his wife rarely reveals a problem in their relationship. It simply means that his primary occasion for prayer is private, not public. Now this is not an excuse for never praying aloud with his wife. We will discuss later in this chapter how couples can pray together. But unless a wife understands her husband's need for private prayer, she will continue to be frustrated and even angry about their corporate prayer time together.

Out of a husband's private prayers to God come a desire and willingness to pray with his wife. So if he never spends time alone with God, then any prayers he may pray with his wife will be empty, contrived, superficial, and hypocritical.

A dear pastor friend of mine loves to get up around five o'clock each morning and pray. He actually retreats into his walk-in bedroom closet, wraps himself in a comforter, puts on his headset from his CD player, listens to worship music, and prays intensely for hours. He never asks his wife to join him. And she has no desire to be there. Why? Because that's his time alone in prayer with the Father.

This pastor loves his wife and prays with her. His intention in his morning prayers is not to exclude his wife but to withdraw from everything and commune with God.

Yes, he often shares with her what God speaks to his heart in prayer. Yes, he intercedes for his wife and family in his private prayers. But his private prayers are just that—private!

Jesus describes such private prayers when He teaches:

> And when you pray, do not be like the hypocrites, for they love to pray standing in the synagogues and on the street corners to be seen by men. I tell you the truth, they have received their reward in full. But when you pray, go into your room, close the door and pray to your Father, who is unseen. Then your Father, who sees what is done in secret [private], will reward you.
>
> —MATTHEW 6:5–6

Jesus points out that our prayers are not for others to hear but solely for God to hear. Such private prayers draw the one praying closer to God. When a man takes the initiative to draw closer to God, then God promises to meet him there. In that private place a man is repentant, purified, cleansed, and humbled. James writes, "Come near to God and he will come near to you. Wash your hands, you sinners, and purify your hearts, you double-minded. Grieve, mourn and wail. Change your laughter to mourning and your joy to gloom. Humble yourselves before the Lord, and he will lift you up" (James 4:8–10).

Without private prayers of repentance and confession, public prayers become arrogant, proud, preachy, and religious. Wives discover that husbands who pray with them publicly without first praying privately may use that prayer time more to preach at them than to talk with God. How humiliating it is to have an arrogant husband, unbroken by God, use prayer to manipulate, correct, judge, and berate his wife!

In a marital counseling session years ago, the wife confessed that she hated praying with her husband. "He preaches at me when we pray," she revealed. "I learn about all my faults, failures, and his unfulfilled expectations of me when we pray. I dread our prayer times together!"

When I asked the husband about his personal quiet time with the Lord, he confessed that he had a hard time with that. In fact, the time he and his wife read the Bible and prayed together was the only time each day he really spent with God. Since he was never broken before the Lord privately, he had nothing to share or minister with his wife in their public prayer time together.

Yes, it is wholesome and healthy for husbands and wives to confess their sins one to another in prayer. "Therefore confess your sins to each other and pray for each other so that you may be healed. The prayer of a righteous man is powerful and effective" (James 5:16). But repentance in private prayer gives a man the strength and courage to share more transparently and become more vulnerable with his wife while praying together.

HIS NEEDS IN PRAYER

OFTEN WIVES CONFIDE to me, "He simply doesn't understand my needs."

"Have you told him?" I ask.

"Told him what?" is the response.

"What your needs are," I inquire.

A look of bewilderment often comes over the spouse's face. She had never considered actually asking for what was needed! Asking for what you need in prayer lays the essential foundation for building a couple's prayer life together. As a couple learns to express their needs to God in prayer, trusting Him to be their source, they will learn to express their needs more openly to one another. People have differing needs spiritually as well as emotionally and physically in a marriage.

So what do husbands need? Do both husbands and wives have the same need to pray together? Every individual will have unique needs. But there are some common needs that I have heard husbands express over the years. Here are a few of those needs:

When husbands pray with their wives, they often need...

1. *Time to think.* That's right! Often husbands complain that their wives suddenly, out of the blue, ask them to pray about something, and they haven't had time to think about it. Now I realize that wives may expect their husbands to be spontaneous, ready-to-pray-at-any-moment prayer warriors. But husbands often like to meditate and reflect on what they pray about. There are occasions for instant, microwave prayer precipitated by emergencies, crises, and immediate needs. But often, if a wife shares a prayer concern and asks her husband to think about it for a while, then when he does pray with her about that need the prayer flows from both his head and his heart.

2. *Time to feel.* Husbands do feel! But their feelings may lie deep beneath the stormy surface of the present gale. Amid the

hurricane that may be raging around him, a husband often must retreat to the eye of the storm for some quiet time to sort out his feelings and emotions about the prayer concern raised by his wife. Such time spent getting in touch with his emotions will bear sensitive fruit when he later prays with his wife.

3. *The right words to pray.* Husbands are often very concerned about saying the right thing. That's not to say that wives are frivolous with words, but men tend to use words more sparingly and deliberately when they pray. While their wives may flow with a fountain of living words that express an ongoing stream of feelings and thoughts, husbands often choose their words carefully for a number of reasons. First, they do not want their wives to misunderstand them. Second, they genuinely desire to be understood and transparent. Finally, they don't want to pay the price of saying the wrong thing and having to apologize later—both to their wives and to God.

4. *A focus or direction for prayer.* One wife reflected, "I just want my husband to pray whatever is on his heart." On the other hand, the husband responded, "I'm not comfortable reaching randomly for things to pray." But when his wife suggested specific areas for prayer in their own lives, marriage, family, and church, he was able to articulate his prayers

focused on her suggestions. When a wife exclaims, "We need to pray," a husband often thinks, *About what?* His lack of an immediate response in prayer does not mean that he feels less of a need to pray than she does. Rather, his thoughts take him beyond the unquestionable need for prayer with his wife to his desire to know what it is that needs prayer. Husbands dislike being put on the spot with a wife's judgment, "Well, you should know what needs prayer." In fact, such a response will usually inhibit a husband from praying with his wife. So when a husband asks, "What do we need to pray about?", then his wife could simply reply, "Will you pray with me about...(naming the prayer need)."

5. *A set time to pray.* This final need is to set a time to pray when both spouses are in the frame of mind to pray. Yes, we should pray without ceasing as Paul instructs (1 Thess. 5:17). But *now* is not always the time when a husband is ready to pray. So if not now, when? A wife can ask her husband to set the time and place for prayer. The time to pray should not be delayed indefinitely. Together make a divine appointment for praying with one another.

The key to prayer at this point in our discussion is simply this: Ask for what you need. If your husband never or rarely brings up his need for praying together, then you be the one who asks for what you need. Refuse to become frustrated or angry over his failure to initiate prayer. As a royal priest in Christ, you have as much right to initiate prayer as he does.

Share your needs and concerns in a nonjudgmental tone. Refuse to put him down for not praying or initiating prayer the way you would like. Instead, ask for what you need; if he still refuses to pray with you, go ahead and pray aloud when he is around to hear you.

Remember that many prayers in the Bible were prayed aloud. How else could they have been heard and recorded by the biblical writers? Let your husband hear you pray aloud. That can effectively communicate to him not only your need to pray with him but also your prayer concerns.

SPIRITUAL CRISIS #2—IS THERE A SPIRITUAL WALL BETWEEN YOU AND YOUR HUSBAND?

COMING HOME FROM church, Mariann turned to Tom and confessed, "I hate going to church when we are such hypocrites." Stunned, Tom reached for the right words to respond. His mind raced through all the possible reasons for her outburst:

> —*Someone said something to hurt her, and she's projecting that pain on to me.*
> —*It's "that time of month" and her hormones are all out of balance.*
> —*She's angry that we were not able to write a tithe check this week because of the unexpected repair bills we had from fixing the van.*
> —*I said something wrong and didn't realize it.*

26

—I should never have agreed to be in that new couples' class. They are always bringing up issues that stir up new spiritual crises and confrontations in our marriage. Maybe it's better to be ignorant of what we are missing out on in our marriage than to be informed. Sometimes, ignorance is bliss!

As his mind raced through these thoughts, a river of tears began to stream down Mariann's cheeks. What seemed to be a wonderful and uplifting worship service had suddenly cascaded into an abyss of hurt and pain—and Tom didn't have a clue as to the reason for the crisis!

At the root of their spiritual crisis in marriage was a spiritual wall that had risen higher and higher between them from years of prayerlessness and the lack of spiritual intimacy. He needed to admit that wall existed. But the only person who could speak the truth in love about that wall was his wife, Mariann.

Now here's the shocker. Wives often hope and pray that someone else will reach their husbands.

They pray for a preacher, teacher, evangelist, prophet, or pastor to say just the right thing and jolt their husbands from spiritual ineptitude. Or they hope one of their husband's friends will say something that will shake him from his prayerlessness. At times, they will even buy books or leave the Bible open to a highlighted verse, hoping to reveal the spiritual problems facing their marriage. A shock jolts a wife when she finally realizes that *she* is the best person to reach her husband and reveal the spiritual wall between them.

Often a wife responds in shocking ways to her husband, and *shock treatment* is usually not the best approach for realizing positive change in a marriage. She may confront, yell, nag, shame, or criticize. She may encourage, plead, beg, or push her husband toward prayer. And while he may change for a season, the sad reality is that lasting change doesn't occur, and after a few weeks or months the spiritual wall reappears stronger and more impregnable than ever.

Wives often wonder aloud in our counseling sessions, "Why does it always have to be *me* who brings up the spiritual problems or needs in our marriage? Doesn't he ever notice that things aren't going right between us spiritually?"

Yes, husbands are without excuse. They should know how important prayer and spiritual discipline is for their marriages.

But the truth usually is that they don't notice the spiritual walls forming between them and their wives because their priorities are misplaced. Jesus clearly set our priorities for life when He taught, "But seek first his kingdom and his righteousness, and all these things will be given to you as well" (Matt. 6:33).

Too often husbands seek first their career goals, financial goals, and family goals. All are important, but they are not the highest priority. Husbands may spend more time trying to please those who care about them least—bosses, clients, or work colleagues—than caring about those who love them most—God, wife, family, and the body of Christ.

Busyness as a result of trying to reach important goals distracts husbands from essential priorities in life, which, simply ranked, are:

—God, first
—Wife and family, next
—Others, following
—Self, last.

Jesus put it this way, "Whoever wants to become great among you must be your servant, and whoever wants to be first must be slave of all" (Mark 10:43–44).

As a husband works and plays harder, involving himself in everything and everyone else before the Lord and his wife, a spiritual wall begins to form between him and his wife.

At first the bricks in the wall are small obstacles on which he stubs his toe and quickly recovers. But later the bricks are cemented together by the mortar of habitual neglect, and a formidable wall is built that requires much repentance to tear down.

In the following chapters, we will expose the bricks in the spiritual walls that develop between husbands and wives who do not pray and share together spiritually. We will also explore biblical, practical ways to break down those walls.

Before discussing the barriers that form spiritual walls, consider taking these initial steps as a wife.

SOME FIRST STEPS
TOWARD BREAKING DOWN THE WALLS

THE FIRST STEP toward breaking down the walls is admitting that we all have needs. Drs. David Ferguson and Don McMinn in their book, *Top Ten Intimacy Needs*, have identified what happens when those needs go unfulfilled. Unfulfilled needs cause us to construct spiritual intimacy walls if we...

▶ *Deny our neediness.* Denial pushes us into self-sufficiency, self-reliance, and insensitivity.

▶ *Exalt our neediness.* Exalting our neediness shapes us into selfish, demanding, and egocentric persons.

▶ *Condemn our neediness.* Condemnation produces frustration and feelings of inferiority.

The following top ten needs for intimacy have been identified through the work of Ferguson and McMinn at The Center for Marriage and Family Intimacy in Austin, Texas:

1. *Acceptance.* "Wherefore, accept one another, just as Christ also accepted us to the glory of God" (Rom. 15:7, NAS).

2. *Approval.* "Because anyone who serves Christ in this way is pleasing to God and approved by men" (Rom. 14:18).

3. *Encouragement.* "Therefore encourage one another and build each other up" (1 Thess. 5:11).

4. *Support/Bear Burdens.* "Carry each other's burdens, and in this way you will fulfill the law of Christ" (Gal. 6:2).

5. *Affection.* "Greet one another with a holy kiss" (Rom. 16:16).

6. *Security.* "May those who love you be secure" (Ps. 122:6).

7. *Respect.* "Show proper respect to everyone" (1 Pet. 2:17).

8. *Attention.* "But that the members [of the body] should have the same care for one another" (1 Cor. 12:25, NAS).

9. *Comfort.* "The God of all comfort, who comforts us in all our troubles, so that we can comfort those in any trouble..." (2 Cor. 1:3–4).
10. *Appreciation.* "I praise you" (1 Cor. 11:2).[2]

Rank these needs in order for yourself, and, if your husband is willing, ask him to rank these needs for himself. Share your findings with one another. Use these lists as prayer lists. If you are not comfortable in asking him to fill out this list, discern how he might rank these needs. Begin praying for your needs and his needs to be met by the God who meets all needs (Phil. 4:19).

> *Heavenly Father, You alone meet every need. I acknowledge that You are my source— not my spouse, my work, my family, or my church. Father, here are my needs...*

In discussing the spiritual walls in marriages with scores of couples, I have discovered that many spouses are willing to allow a wall to remain. Why?

1. *Denial.* They refuse to admit it's there. Their sin deceives them and leads them down the destructive path of denial.
2. *Ignorance.* They do not know that they can have a deeper, more meaningful relationship in marriage through prayer and spiritual discipline. And they do not know any new, fresh, real, and genuine ways to begin praying and growing spiritually together.

3. *Pain.* They are unwilling to risk the pain and effort it will take to achieve spiritual gain in their marriage.

4. *Lack of faith.* They simply do not believe that they can change. Often the wife has tried for years to make her husband change through prayer, nagging, threats, withdrawal, criticism, and encouragement. In other words, she feels she has tried everything and nothing has worked. So why keep trying? Why kick a dead horse? So she sacrifices prayer and spirituality on the altar of "keeping peace."

5. *Fear.* The wife fears that breaking down the spiritual wall might reveal a husband less appealing than the one she now knows. Or she may fear becoming vulnerable again to hurt. She may fear rejection and failure. The husband, on the other hand, may fear exposing his own spiritual poverty or barrenness. He may fear that his wife is simply going to manipulate his feelings or attitudes to "get what she wants." Or he may fear admitting his past failures and having to change.

So, you may ask, "What can I do that I have not already done so that my husband will pray with me and desire to grow spiritually with me?"

You've taken the first step by admitting there is a problem—a spiritual wall does exist.

Second Timothy 1:7 enlightens you to your next step: "God did not give us a spirit of timidity, but a spirit of power, of love and of self-discipline."

Let me share a final word of practical encouragement before you turn the pages and examine each of the bricks that may be in your spiritual wall.

The pages of Scripture are filled with prayers. How did they get there? Someone either wrote them down or prayed them aloud. Silent prayers are heard by God but not by others.

Jesus' prayer in John 17 was heard by His disciples and later written down for us to hear. Take these positive steps:

▶ *Pray aloud.* Do not be afraid to let your husband hear and read your prayers.
▶ *Write your prayers down.*
▶ *Don't pray sermons.* Do not use prayer to preach at your husband.
▶ *Keep your prayers simple.* In the morning, at meals, before going to sleep at night, say a simple prayer to God in the hearing of your husband.

What might you pray for your husband? Here is a suggestion:

> *Lord Jesus, reveal to my husband my love for him. Break down the spiritual walls between us and help us to pray together. Change us, Lord.*
>
> *—Amen*

Don't expect your husband to respond. Since you are not praying to him, then you have no expectation for anyone to answer your prayer but God. Good news! God will answer, and the walls will come tumbling down.

INITIAL INSIGHTS FOR BREAKING DOWN SPIRITUAL WALLS

IN THIS CHAPTER we have discovered that . . .

- ❯ Christ is the High Priest of a marriage and family. Both husbands and wives are priests and intercessors for their families.
- ❯ Husbands and wives are servant-leaders in the home—serving one another through prayer and ministry. Prayer fosters service, and service leads a couple back to prayer.
- ❯ Men need to develop their private, intimate, personal prayer lives before they can pray effectively with their wives.
- ❯ When husbands pray with their wives, they often need time to think, time to feel, the right words to pray, a focus or direction for prayer, and a set time to pray.
- ❯ Spiritual walls are often constructed as the result of a husband's misplaced priorities in marriage.
- ❯ Often the best person to reach a husband spiritually is his wife.
- ❯ Husbands and/or wives are unwilling at times to break down spiritual walls because of denial, ignorance, pain, lack of faith, or fear.
- ❯ The desire to tear down spiritual walls is necessary and healthy in a marriage. When either spouse is willing to admit there is a wall and is willing to tear it down, that person has nothing to fear, hide, or lose.
- ❯ One way to begin pulling down the walls that separate husbands and wives in prayer is for a wife to begin praying aloud so that her husband can hear her prayers.

●●●

YOU HAVE NOTHING TO FEAR, NOTHING TO HIDE, AND NOTHING TO LOSE. GOD IS GIVING YOU THE POWER TO DO SOMETHING ABOUT THE WALL. HE IS ALSO GIVING YOU THE LOVE FOR YOUR HUSBAND THAT YOU NEED. GOD LOVES BOTH OF YOU SO MUCH THAT HE WILL NOT LET YOU STAY WHERE YOU ARE— HE LOVES YOU ENOUGH TO CHANGE YOU! YOU CAN PERSEVERE AND PATIENTLY PERSIST IN TAKING POSITIVE STEPS TO TEAR DOWN THE WALL.

●●●

Begin praying:

Lord Jesus, I confess there is a spiritual wall between my husband and me. I ask You for the self-discipline, courage, power, and love to work at breaking the wall down.

I know that You love me enough to protect me, to give me the right words to say, and to change both my husband and me.

I will begin today to pray daily for my husband. Help me, Lord, to be a priest, prayer warrior, and godly wife.

In Jesus' name.

—Amen

Now turn the page. Start removing the bricks from the spiritual walls between you and your husband.

Take from me all that hinders and teach me to accept in its place all that You accept: the ceaseless demands, needs, conflicts, pressures, misunderstandings even of those who love You best.

—Evelyn Underhill
19th–20th Century a.d.

3

Breaking Down the
Spiritual Walls of...

UNFULFILLED EXPECTATIONS, UNIMPLEMENTED PLANS, AND UNKEPT PROMISES

THE WALL OF UNFULFILLED EXPECTATIONS

BEFORE JOANN AND Will were married, they spent most of their courtship involved in church ministry. As high school sweethearts, they were leaders in the youth group; both felt called to full-time ministry. Both began attending the local community college to save money toward their junior year when they planned to go to Bible school. However, their courtship evolved into engagement and resulted in marriage after both had received their associate's degrees.

Joann decided to work full time to help pay for Will's school. He decided to go for his teaching degree as a way to earn a living and then go on to Bible school later. But later never came.

After two children and an accumulation of debt for cars, house, and furniture, Will and Joann settled for just a memory of ministry and devoted as much time as possible to teaching Sunday school and volunteering in children's ministry at church.

While Will became increasingly involved in a multitude of tasks—teaching, coaching, men's ministry, and doing home repair work in the summer for extra money, Joann began to brood over lost dreams. She remembered the extended quiet times and long hours of prayer she and Will had shared before marriage. It seemed as if marriage had changed everything. Will no longer seemed interested in praying with her or reading the Bible. The spiritual intimacy they had enjoyed in college had been squeezed out of their lives by work, raising children, and running to and fro to a multitude of activities. Even ministry at church seemed more of a duty than a joy.

We had dinner one evening with Will and Joann, never suspecting the brewing volcano beneath the surface. They had always been enthusiastic volunteers at church and were regarded as low-maintenance parishioners. But as we visited over dinner about all the superficial issues that swirled around us, Joann suddenly blurted out her frustration. "Will we ever get time to spend time again with God? Do you ever recover what you lose when you drift away from God?"

Will gazed at his spaghetti, refusing to look at anyone.

My wife and I simply tried to change the subject, thinking to ourselves, *Do pastors and their wives ever get an evening off? Must we always talk about spiritual issues?*

As a pastor, I confess to the secret desire to relate to people who have no idea we are in the ministry. Like doctors who must give free diagnoses outside of the office, so ministers are expected to be available whenever someone needs counsel or spiritual guidance. But this casual dinner engagement with this lay couple in our church was destined to become a cathartic time of unloading feelings that we had to handle in a sensitive, pastoral way.

Joann's frustration was actually much deeper than her comment revealed. And it was a divine appointment to begin talking with them about the spiritual wall of unfulfilled expectations.

As they shared, it became evident that their hopes and dreams for being in ministry had succumbed to the reality of making a living and raising a family. Not only had Will failed to live up to Joann's expectations, but God had as well. Her repressed anger at both boiled over as she lamented all the ways Will and God had fallen short of her dreams for ministry.

As Joann shared, Will withdrew into an uneasy silence and offered no defense or rebuttal to her teary accusations. Obviously he had heard her laments many times before and had long since given up trying to approach any spiritual issue with his wife.

Finally, after the flood of her feelings had subsided, I began to probe his feelings. He shared that he had long since stopped trying to pray with his wife or share spiritually since each attempt always ended with a litany of all his past failures, centering on his ministry failures. A spiritual wall of unfulfilled expectations had risen like Mount Rainier between them, and they did not even have the faith of a mustard seed to remove it.

The spiritual wall of unfulfilled expectations between husbands and wives can be understood in light of a revelatory story in the Old Testament. Go with me behind the scenes of David's first marriage to Michal, King Saul's daughter.

EVEN GODLY MEN CAN DISAPPOINT THEIR WIVES

DAVID WAS DESCRIBED as a man after God's own heart (1 Sam. 13:14). King Saul's daughter, Michal, loved David and became his first wife. What a spiritual union this should have been! Michal and her older sister, Merab, were the first princesses in the history of Israel. Michal married Israel's hero, David, who had slain Goliath and killed thousands of the hated enemies of Israel, the Philistines.

The daughter of the first anointed king of Israel, Michal, marries the anointed poet, psalmist, warrior, and soon-to-be-king David. She protects David from Saul's moody fits of rage that prompt Saul to attempt to murder David at every opportunity. Every reference to Michal before David flees from Saul refers to her protective love for David. (See 1 Samuel 18:20, 28; 19:11–18.)

The day comes when King Saul and his son Jonathan—David's beloved friend—are slain during a battle with the Philistines. David moves skillfully to secure the throne, being first anointed king over Judah, and then over Israel. (See 2 Samuel 2 and 5.)

What has happened to Michal? Now the plot thickens. Earlier David fled from Saul's murderous persecutions, Saul had given Michal in marriage to Paltiel, while David married Abigail and Ahinoam. (See 1 Samuel 25:43–44.) After David was anointed king of all of Israel, he asked for Michal to return to him (2 Sam. 3:14–15). She is taken from her second husband, Paltiel, and returned to David's household.

Curiously, no mention is made to any love or intimacy between Michal and David.

The next scene featuring King David and Michal is staged when David brings the ark to Jerusalem, leaping and dancing before the Lord. "But as the Ark of the LORD entered the City of David, Michal, the daughter of Saul, looked down from her window. When she saw King David leaping and dancing before the LORD, she was filled with contempt for him" (2 Sam. 6:16, NLT).

Consider the unfulfilled expectations Michal may have harbored for David. David abandoning her for two other women had betrayed her expressed love for him. Having found some refuge in a marriage to Paltiel, Michal is taken from her weeping husband, who obviously loved her, and returned to King David (2 Sam. 3:15–16). Does David shower Michal with love and attention? No. Does he even notice her? Nothing indicates he does. In fact, David proceeds to take more concubines and wives for himself in Jerusalem and bears more children while apparently ignoring his first wife, Michal (2 Sam. 5:13–16). When it came to marriage and marital fidelity, David was simply a lout.

Something happened within Michal. Perhaps it was caused by David's first abandonment and marriage to other women. Or it may have been generated by his tearing away of Michal from Paltiel. Or David's continual philandering with women in Jerusalem right in front of Michal may have finally pushed her to build a spiritual wall that not only came between her and her husband but also between her and God.

As David danced and leaped in worship, praise,

and joy before the Ark of God, Michal despised, scorned, felt contempt for, and viewed David as a vile person (2 Sam. 6:16).

Her unfulfilled expectations for him as a husband or spiritual leader blinded her from recognizing that his dancing was indeed before the Lord and not a lewd display for the women of Israel. She could see his dancing only as vulgar. The spiritual wall of unfulfilled expectations between David and her clouded her judgment of him in spiritual matters and left her barren—both physically and spiritually.

Yes, the way David treated her was wrong and inexcusable. His marriage and family life would remain in shambles all his life. But David still had a heart for God—something that Michal could not recognize or discern because of her spiritual wall of unfulfilled expectations.

Michal's love for David was conditional. When he fulfilled certain expectations or conditions, she loved him. But let David fail to meet her conditions and her love was withdrawn.

People who have strings attached to their love have conditional love. In the Greek language four words are often translated *love*. *Agape* is God's love, which is unconditional, accepting, and seeks out the best for the one loved. *Storge* is natural affection, like the love between parents and children or siblings or relatives. *Eros* is physical desire or lust, while *philos* is brotherly love, most commonly expressed when people are working together for a common goal. All forms of love except *agape* are conditional love.

At times, the most difficult people to love with

unconditional love are those who have conditional love for you. Why? Those who love conditionally are always extending or withdrawing love based on feelings or circumstances. They can become legalistic and often use guilt to manipulate others.

If you are loving your husband conditionally with a number of expectations tied to your love, then he will find it hard to love you unconditionally. And unconditional love, *agape,* is the very love that you need! What you need the most you may be repelling by your own conditional, or selfish, form of love. Michal's demanding, controlling, conditional love loaded with expectations drove the one she desired away from her. Your expectations may be doing the same thing to your husband. If you have conditional love, you could well be building a wall between your husband and you.

Conditional love can be expressed in spiritual terms. You may say to your husband or imply by your actions that...

- ❯ If you [husband] do not pray with me [your wife], then I will not love you.
- ❯ If you do not become the spiritual head of our home, then I cannot love you unconditionally.
- ❯ If you do not love me unconditionally, then I will not love you unconditionally.

WHAT BUILDS THE SPIRITUAL WALL OF UNFULFILLED EXPECTATIONS?

THE WALL BETWEEN Will and Joann had been built with the bricks of shattered hopes and dreams for ministry. Between Michal and David a wall of unfulfilled expectations for marital love and commitment had arisen. Have unfulfilled expectations formed a wall between you and your husband?

The root cause of unfulfilled expectations lies in our desire for others to be created in our image of them. We often expect our spouse to be or become someone they are not or ever will be.

A wife may marry the vision of the man she hopes her husband will become instead of accepting the real life portrait of who her husband really is. The day inevitably arrives when she wakes up and discovers that the man lying next to her is not a mighty man of God but merely a bearded idol with clay feet and horns instead of a halo.

In other circumstances, a couple may go through courtship and even the early years of marriage being faithfully committed to prayer, devotions, and sharing spiritually. They may even feel that they have a call from God to enter into full-time Christian ministry. However, as the years pass, the spiritual intimacy grows shallow and the frequency of prayer becomes sporadic until it ceases altogether. Realizing her profound spiritual loss, a wife may begin to nag, cajole, shame, or prod her husband into returning to the glory days of old. Invariably her efforts to fan flames of spiritual passion from cold embers fail, and she builds a spiritual wall of unfulfilled expectations between herself and her husband.

Of course, not only wives build such walls. A husband who expects his wife to be more encouraging, supportive, and accepting when he enters into times of spiritual backsliding discovers she does just the opposite. Instead of praying for him, she judges, criticizes, and condemns him for his spiritual weaknesses. As an end result, the husband erects a spiritual wall of unfulfilled expectations, if for no other reason than to shield himself—albeit inadequately—from her relentless attacks.

All the explanations in the world for why the expectations went unfulfilled do little to break down the wall that they build. So, let's zero in on:

> ➤ What tempts a wife to build a wall of unfulfilled expectations?
> ➤ How does a wife determine if such a wall exists and how strong it may be?
> ➤ What practical steps can she take to avoid building the wall of unfulfilled expectations?

HOW STRONG IS YOUR WALL OF UNFULFILLED EXPECTATIONS?

YOUR HUSBAND MAY not fulfill all your spiritual expectations of him. And yes, you may have some negative feelings and responses as a result. But don't take the bait of Satan. What is it? John Bevere, in his book *The Bait of Satan,* describes the bait as taking up an offense against the other person. You will be tempted to take up an offense. Once you take the bait of offense, a wall of separation forms between you and your husband. Bevere observes astutely:

> If I have expectations about certain persons, those people can let me down. They will disappoint me to the degree they fall short of my expectations. But if I have no expectations about someone, anything given is a blessing

45

and not something owed. We set ourselves up for offense when we require certain behaviors from those with whom we have relationships. The more we expect, the greater the potential offense.[1]

The greater your expectation of your husband to pray, the greater you are offended when he fails to pray as often or as deeply as you expect. The greater your expectation of your husband to take spiritual leadership in your home, the greater your offense will be when he fails to take leadership—even when he does show spiritual maturity in some areas but fails miserably in others just as David did.

How can you avoid unrealistic expectations? Is it possible to surrender all the spiritual expectations you have for your husband? Is Bevere being realistic when he urges us not to have expectations of others? Absolutely!

Husbands and wives will offend one another both intentionally and unintentionally. Jesus observed, "It is impossible that no offenses should come." (See Luke 17:1.) We should put a bumper sticker on our marriage limos that reads *Offenses Happen!* Offenses will happen, but how you respond to the offenses determines whether or not a spiritual wall will go up in your marriage.

You can expect your husband to be what God expects him—and you—to be. In our natural, carnal, unsaved condition, God knows we are:

➤ Deceitfully wicked (Jer. 17:9)
➤ Blind and foolish (Rom. 1:21–23)
➤ Always falling short (Rom. 3:23)

46

➤ Powerless (Rom. 5:6)
➤ Cursed (Gal. 3:10)
➤ Corrupted by deceitful desires (Eph. 4:22)
➤ Proud enemies of God (James 4:4–10)

But wait, you protest. My husband is a Christian. Can't I expect higher and nobler things of him now?

God can, but you cannot. "We who are strong ought to bear with the failings of the weak and not to please ourselves...Accept one another, then, just as Christ accepted you, in order to bring praise to God" (Rom. 15:1, 7). God changes our mates; we don't. *God* is making our spouses into new creations, but *we* cannot make them into anything (2 Cor. 5:17).

God is transforming your husband into the man He desires him to be, and He doesn't need your help (2 Cor. 3:18). God simply wants your prayers. That transformation may not be happening soon enough for your liking. If that's the case, then ask yourself, *Am I willing to wait on God to change my husband even if it takes a lifetime of prayer and patience?* Remember that God is the change agent. We are the prayer agents. E. M. Bounds reflects, "All God's saints came to their sainthood by the way of prayer. The saints could do nothing without prayer."[2]

The keys to avoiding the temptation to build a spiritual wall of unfulfilled expectations between you and your husband are:

1. See your husband as God sees him.
2. Accept your husband as Christ has accepted him.
3. Pray continually for your husband.
4. Wait and watch for God to change him.

47

Years ago I was co-leading a youth workers' retreat with Carol and Dave. Each afternoon of the retreat we would meet with the youth leaders individually to answer any private or personal concerns that they had in ministry and to pray with them.

Carol and I talked with a woman who tearfully shared about her husband who had no concern for spiritual things. He never went to church with her. He never encouraged the children to pray or to read their Bibles.

In fact, he ridiculed her spirituality in front of the children. She had prayed for him and his salvation throughout their fifteen years of marriage, and her patience was wearing dangerously thin. Like a rope frayed to its last thread, this wife was barely holding on to marriage. She confided to us that she was seriously considering filing for a divorce when she returned home.

This wife described how her husband would actually hinder the family from worshiping by planning family outings and fun activities on Sunday mornings. As his wife urged the children to get dressed for church, he would try to entice them to go with him to a picnic, the beach, or on a bike ride. Besides, he was crude and rude. He often put down his wife in front of the children and left soft porn magazines laying around for everyone in the house to see. I listened quietly as Carol engaged this hurting wife with some sensitive questions. Carol asked, "Are you praying for your husband?"

"Yes," replied the wife. "I'm praying for God to change him."

"Why not start praying a different kind of prayer?" encouraged Carol.

"Like what?" the women inquired. "Maybe like, 'God, take him out'?"

"That's not quite what I had in mind. Why not start praying for God to save him?"

"Oh, I used to pray that, but I've given up. I think he's impossible. He'll never repent and turn to God," grieved the wife.

Then Carol probed deeper. "So what are you going to do?"

"I'm tired of waiting on my husband and God. The children and I would be better off without him. I'm considering filing divorce papers when I return," the wife answered with anger lacing every word.

"Are you willing to wait on God to save your husband?" asked Carol.

"How long?" she shot back.

"As long as it takes . . . maybe a lifetime," Carol counseled.

So, if your husband isn't all that you expect, are you willing to pray and wait a lifetime for God to change him?

▶ *Repenting of the Wall of Unfulfilled Expectations* ◀

Lord Jesus, You alone can destroy and shatter my wall of unfulfilled expectations. I repent of building this wall in my marriage. I repent of the times I have allowed this wall to rob us of joy and love.

Lord Jesus, I repent of expecting my spouse to meet my needs, which only You can meet. Forgive me for having unrealistic, irrational, unreachable expectations. Forgive me for the angry emotions I have felt and the hurtful things I have said when my expectations were not met by my mate. Forgive me for the times I have put him/her down in front of others because he/she has not fulfilled my expectations.

Lord Jesus, I repent of the selfishness I have expressed by expecting and wanting things from others when You alone are my strength and source. Thank You, Lord Jesus, for giving me the person you gave as my mate.

Help me to express my needs in ways that communicate with no condemnation or criticism.

In Jesus' name, I now repent and declare that my wall of unfulfilled expectations is destroyed and abolished. I praise God that He is willing and able to meet all of my needs in Christ Jesus.

I receive His forgiveness, peace, and power to resist the temptation to rebuild this wall in the future. I ask my spouse to forgive me.

—Amen

M

In unison read aloud Philippians 4:19–20.

And this same God who takes care of me will supply all your needs from his glorious riches, which have been given to us in Christ Jesus. Now glory be to God our Father forever and ever. Amen.

—NLT

THE WALL OF UNIMPLEMENTED PLANS

TERESA LONGED FOR a stable home and ministry partnership in her marriage. Her husband wanted stability and a fixed direction in their marriage, but nothing seemed to work. They came to share with me about their frustrations.

"Every home we plan to buy has fallen through in the past few years," Teresa complained.

"My sales income fluctuates so much that it's hard to get approved for a mortgage," confided Sam. "We zero in on a home, put in a contract, and begin to dream about where all our furniture will fit. We commit our plans to God. Doesn't the Bible promise to give us the desires of our hearts when we commit our way to God?"

As their plans fell apart one after another, Teresa and Sam's prayer life together crumbled. They had become accustomed to praying together when they needed or wanted something from God, but seeing hope after hope disintegrate had eroded their prayers like acid burns through metal. What had been an ironclad prayer life had rusted into a shambles of dreams abandoned like rusting wrecks in a junkyard.

Teresa shared, "My faith, both in my husband and in God, has been shaken. I have been taught that when two agree together in faith, God acts. We are agreed. We have faith, but God isn't coming through. What are we doing wrong? Is there sin in our lives? Do we need more faith? Should we be doing more for God? What do we do next?"

Sam and Teresa had hit the wall. All of the simple and easy prayer remedies for their lives had been exhausted. Now they had stopped praying and started doubting God and themselves. Their next step would be disillusionment. Why? When we pray for our illusions, we will reap a harvest of disillusionment.

The wall of unimplemented plans arises when we expect God to bless our plans instead of our blessing God for His plan. Instead of planning our work and then working the plan, we need to be seeking God for His plan, dreams, and visions. Our plans are often strategies to meet our wants instead of doing what God wants. We may disguise our selfish motives with religious piety and language like the Pharisees and religious leaders when they prayed (Luke 18:9–14). Jesus rebuked their prideful attitudes in prayer and commended humility, "For everyone who exalts himself will be humbled, and he who humbles himself will be exalted" (Luke 18:14).

To avoid the wall of unimplemented plans, I encourage you to...

1. *Seek God with your husband for His plan.* We used to plan our futures by taking a yellow legal pad and listing all the pros and cons to a decision. If the pros outnumbered the cons then it must be God's will, and vice versa. However, nowhere in Scripture does it say that legal pads are good devices for discerning God's will. It does say to listen to Scripture, God's voice in prayer, the counsel of wise believers, the witness of the Spirit in your heart, the evidence of God's peace in your life, and the way God is moving in circumstances

to test God's will. Is the plan before you God's best, God's way, in God's timing, and for His glory? If it meets every test but one, then take time out. Do not rush into a plan that looks like a good idea but fails to be God's idea.

2. *Refuse to settle for less than His plan.* Do not fix your faith in your husband's plan, your plan, or even those plans you agree upon for yourselves.

3. *Be open to God's Spirit who gives us both dreams and visions.* (See Joel 2; Acts 2.)

4. *Believe that the plans God has for you are good, not evil.* God declares, "'For I know the plans I have for you,' declares the LORD, 'plans to prosper you and not to harm you, plans to give you hope and a future. Then you will call upon me and come and pray to me, and I will listen to you. You will seek me and find me when you seek me with all your heart'" (Jer. 29:11–13).

5. *Stop trying and start trusting.* Legalism and religion seek to implement plans without God's power and strength. Prayer recognizes that implementing God's plans does not depend on our strength but His. "'Not by might nor by power, but by my Spirit,' says the LORD Almighty" (Zech. 4:6).

6. *Failing doesn't make you or your husband a failure.* Too often couples give up on God's plans when things—from their perspectives—go wrong. But temporary

setbacks or failures do not mean that the plans will never be implemented. If God is in it, then don't give up! If you could accomplish the plan, it would not be God. He goes beyond our strength and resources to accomplish the impossible. Jesus advises us, "With man this is impossible, but with God all things are possible" (Matt. 19:26).

7. *Stop expecting spiritual growth in marriage to be easy. Easy* rarely appears in God's vocabulary. It is easy for one who has God's understanding, and Jesus' yoke of salvation is easy for the believer (Prov. 14:6; Matt. 11:30). But life isn't easy. Jesus warns, "In this world you will have trouble. But take heart! I have overcome the world" (John 16:33). Hence, give your faith muscles a workout; you may be in for some power lifting, but when God is in it, nothing can stop His plan but you!

8. *Write it down!* When God gives a plan, vision, or dream to you or your husband, or to both of you, then write it down. "Write the vision," God instructs Habbakkuk (Hab. 2:2, KJV). Write down whatever plan the Lord gives you, and then pray over that plan aloud together. If your husband will not pray with you, then write it down yourself. Put it on the refrigerator with magnets. Write it on the mirror in the bathroom. Speak it aloud when you pray in your husband's hearing. Never quit on God's plan!

▶ *Repenting of the Wall of Unimplemented Plans* ◀

Lord Jesus, I repent for having my plans, not Yours . . . my ideas, not Yours . . . my visions and dreams, not Yours . . . and expecting my mate to implement them. I know, Lord, that You have placed in our lives wonderful plans for us and given us awesome dreams and visions by Your Spirit.

But I also know, Lord Jesus, that I have sought my best, not Your best; in my way, not Your way; and according to my timing, not Your timing. Forgive me, Christ Jesus.

Lord, for those times we have made plans together and my mate has not followed through on his/her responsibilities, I forgive him/her. And Lord, I ask Your forgiveness for any resentment, anger, frustrations, and angry words that I have expressed.

Jesus, take all my unfinished plans, broken dreams, and blurred visions out of my life so that I may be uncluttered and free to receive all that You have for us in our marriage. Send Your Holy Spirit to guide, direct, instruct, and empower us to follow Your plans.

In Jesus' name, I ask forgiveness and declare that my wall of unimplemented plans is abolished by the grace and power of Christ. I praise God that we can start over and plan anew in His will, way, and timing. I thank You, Lord, for giving us a second chance, and I receive Your forgiveness. I ask my mate to forgive me and join with me in seeking Your plans for our future together in You.

Jesus, by faith we receive Your promise that Your plans for us are for good—not disaster, to give us a future and a hope in You. Jesus, be the planner of our marriage.

—Amen

M

In unison, real aloud Jeremiah 29:11–13.

"For I know the plans I have for you," says the LORD. "They are plans for good and not for disaster, to give you a future and a hope. In those days when you pray, I will listen. If you look for me in earnest, you will find me when you seek me."

—NLT

THE WALL OF UNKEPT PROMISES

TENS OF THOUSANDS of men fill stadiums across the country. Over a million men gather to pray in Washington. They are called Promise Keepers. Around the nation, men are rededicating themselves to keep the promises they make to God, their wives, their families, their churches, and at work. But what happens to prayer in a marriage when the husband fails to keep a promise?

Again, without God's Spirit and strength it is humanly impossible to keep a promise. The only perfect Promise Keeper is God. But when a husband has promised one thing and does another, his credibility and integrity with his wife takes a severe hit. How can you keep from building a wall from the bricks of unkept promises when your husband breaks his word?

Lee was the model husband and layman at church. He followed through on every commitment. His family felt loved and secure. But Lee had a deep need inside that his wife could not meet. One day without warning he announced to Brenda that he didn't love her anymore and was going to move out.

Yes, he was a hard worker. In fact, he held down two jobs while balancing his church ministry and family responsibilities. He tried hard to make as many of his son's basketball games as possible. But his wife always seemed to overshadow him in spiritual leadership. Though both were prominent leaders in the couples' ministry, she always seemed to be the one making the speeches and organizing the events. He quietly followed her lead.

After he left Brenda, I visited with her and the four children. They were stunned and puzzled by his actions. The best that anyone could guess was that he had simply burned out from overwork and financial stress.

Then I talked with Lee. He made few excuses for walking out of the marriage. He stated simply that he was tired and stressed out by bills, his wife's desire for more and more stuff, and his lack of calling to do ministry to the extent his wife wanted him involved in Christian work.

Tragically, one of Brenda's alleged friends told her not to look back. With Lee out of the way she would be free to do ministry and get on with her own spiritual maturing. A cold chill froze my sensitivities as I heard this remark. Such a perspective brought back painful memories in my own life.

Years before, my wife and I had faced serious marital problems. My overwork and lack of attention to her and the children had built a wall between us. Time and time again I promised to work less, spend more time with her and the family, and to devote myself more to praying with her and reading the Word with her and the children. I taught others how to pray with their wives and children while breaking my promises to my own family to pray with them. Most nights I arrived home after their prayer times when they were already in bed. Nights on end my wife, Judi, would cry herself to sleep.

Hoping to remedy the situation, I worked harder at keeping my promises and failed more miserably. My actions drove my wife further and further away from me. The wall of unkept promises was so impenetrable that every time I made a promise, Judi would feel the fiery darts of all the previous unkept promises. A promise on my lips was a source of pain—not hope or comfort.

I went to a Christian counselor hoping to find some answers. Unwisely, he counseled me to divorce. He felt the wall between us was impenetrable. In the words of an old chorus, the wall of unkept promises between Judi and me was "so high you couldn't get over it, so low you couldn't get under it, and so wide you couldn't go around it." But the closing words of the chorus provided just the hope I needed: "You have to go through the door!"

I failed to heed the words of that counselor—one

of the wisest failures I had in those years! Instead, I began to seek Christ for guidance and strength. He was the door I needed to go through. In fact, His door was like the proverbial eye of the needle. I had to humble myself in order to go through it. The only way to destroy the wall of unkept promises was through repentance and humility. In His grace and faithfulness God restored my relationship with my teenage daughter and kept my wife praying for me even when we could not pray together. A year later God dealt with my heart and began to tear down the wall between us.

Even if you have given up on your husband whose promises you can no longer trust, don't give up on Christ. All His promises are *yes* and *amen* (2 Cor. 1:20). In other words, He keeps His promises even when your husband cannot.

In the Old Testament, Ruth never gave up on God's provisions for her, and God provided a godly husband, Boaz. And when Elkanah could not promise Hannah a child, she turned to God and discovered that He was faithful (1 Samuel 1). There is one completely reliable Promise Keeper in your family. His name is Jesus. When the groom fails to keep his promises, turn to the Bridegroom whose promises never fail.

Promise keeping is a matter of trust in a marriage. When trust has been violated and trampled in the dirt like a used and abused rag, then pick it up and take your trust to the Promise Keeper—Christ. Pray. Ask Him to do what is humanly impossible—to rebuild the trust between you and your husband.

Remember Lee and Brenda? They had a very difficult task in breaking down their wall of unkept promises because he left the relationship and she decided that her ministry was too important to her. So he went his way and she went hers, without either person making a move toward one another in trust.

So how does the wall get torn down and trust rebuilt?

- ❯ Stay in the relationship. Refuse to allow unkept promises to destroy the relationship.
- ❯ Begin to pray the promises of God for your marriage and for your husband. First pray through your marriage vows. For example: "Lord, I promise to love my mate through sickness and health, through poverty and riches, for better or for worse, as long as we both shall live. Amen."
- ❯ Affirm your husband when he keeps a promise, and refuse to condemn him when he fails. In counseling I often ask couples to recount for me the number of good and bad days they have had in the preceding week. They might say, "Well, Monday and Tuesday were okay, but Wednesday everything fell apart. Thursday was ruined as a result of Wednesday, but Friday and Saturday went okay. Then we got into a terrible fight on Sunday." Then I remind them that four out of seven days were good days for their marriage. That's a majority! In fact, in baseball a hitter is considered great when he only gets a hit one out of three times. In other words, he fails two out of every three times at bat and is a huge success. So cherish every good day, and release the bad days.
- ❯ Start small. Jesus says that when we are faithful in a little, then we can be entrusted with much

(Luke 19:17). Talk with your husband about small promises both of you can keep with one another, and then move to bigger things. His grace is sufficient one day at a time. Keep your marriage vows one day at a time, and you will not have to worry about keeping them for a lifetime.

▶ Finally, be accountable. Tell your husband when you break a promise, and then ask his forgiveness. Ask him to do the same. Pray forgiveness over one another aloud. Don't just tell your partner that you're sorry or that you will forgive. Pray your confession or forgiveness aloud for God and your husband to hear.

▶ *Repenting of the Wall of Unkept Promises* ◀

Jesus, I know that all of God's promises in You are yes and amen. I repent for expecting my mate to keep every promise he/she has made, knowing that he/she is not perfect.

Lord, it is only by Your power and grace that any of us can become promise keepers. So Jesus, help my mate to keep the promises that he/she makes, and help me to forgive and understand when he/she fails. And may that same grace be extended to me when I fail to keep my promises.

Heavenly Father, You have promised to be my security. It is in You and not in others that I place my trust and hope. Enable me to make and keep promises that are rooted in Your will and Word.

Lord, we commit our way to You and

trust You to implement every plan, vision, and dream that comes by Your Spirit. You, O Lord, are my delight, and my heart is fixed on You. In Jesus' name, demolish the wall of unkept promises and heal all hurts from disappointments and disillusionments caused by unkept promises in the past.
In Jesus' name.

—Amen

M

With your spouse, read this verse aloud:

For no matter how many promises God has made, they are "Yes" in Christ. And so through him the "Amen" is spoken by us to the glory of God.

—2 CORINTHIANS 1:20

A HUSBAND'S PERSPECTIVE

HUSBANDS THAT FACE walls of unfulfilled expectations, unimplemented plans, and unkept promises may view the walls with different perspectives than their wives. When facing those walls, I've heard some husbands say:

- ❯ I feel as though the harder I try the more I fail to reach my wife's expectations.
- ❯ My failures always seem to be counted, but my successes are never noticed.
- ❯ When I keep my promises, no one in the family seems to appreciate it or thank me. But let me

62

break a promise and everyone makes me the goat.

❯ My wife has unrealistic expectations of me. I have given up trying to do the impossible. Only Jesus could please her, and then only on certain days.

❯ I cannot fulfill all my wife's needs. But she refuses to reach out and make friends with others. How do we build a support network with other believers?

❯ When we pray together, she tells God what she wants of me and what I haven't done. I feel exposed and ridiculed in front of God when we pray.

❯ When we make plans I don't want to disappoint my wife, so I just agree with whatever she wants. But when it doesn't happen, I get blamed as a failure.

❯ My wife feels that I am content with less than God's best for me or His excellence.

❯ Because I don't claim the promises of God the way my wife does in prayer, she sees me as lacking faith. She calls my realism unbelief.

❯ I am much slower making decisions than my wife. So she views me as indecisive and ambivalent.

❯ I will never be the kind of husband my wife expects me to be, so I've just given up and simply do the best I can.

Does your husband have any of these feelings or observations? Take time to read through them with your husband. After sharing, pray aloud together in unison:

Lord Jesus, empower us to understand Your expectations of us. Mold our expectations of each other by Your will. Help us to surrender our personal expectations of one another to Your will for us as a couple. Thank You for answering our prayer.

—Amen

THE BRIDEGROOM'S PERSPECTIVE

JESUS EVALUATES US based on our faithfulness to what has been entrusted to us. Husbands and wives often get into the trap of comparing themselves or their spouses to other couples. In defending himself, a husband may protest, "Well, I pray with you more than John prays with his wife." Or a wife may critically say, "I wish you could be as spiritual as William is in his marriage. Mary tells me they pray together daily in the morning and evening. They really share deeply in their spiritual lives. I wish we could get to where they are."

Jesus revealed that to one person is given five talents, to another is given two, and still another has one. To each person God gives according to that person's ability (Matt. 25:14–30). So a spouse cannot expect five-talent performance out of a two-talent person. Yes, God is no respecter of persons. Notice that He does not degrade the two-talent person for only earning two talents instead of five. He measures our performance based on the abilities and talents He has created within us—not in comparison to others. And He rewards those who serve Him faithfully without discrimination (Matt. 20:8). But for those who are not faithful to what He has entrusted them, God judges them harshly.

Not all husbands and wives find themselves at the

same place spiritually. For some, a sentence prayer reflects the depth God desires from their hearts while others may pray for hours without pause. For them to pray less would be lack of faithfulness to what God has given them.

God accepts us where we are and loves us too much to leave us there. We do not grow in comparison to our spouses or other couples. We mature in our relationships to the level of relationship we have with our ultimate standard, who is Christ.

Don't expect your husband to pray like a preacher or elder if he is not one. Don't be drawn into the trap of comparing your husband to others. Rather, affirm his heart's desire to grow spiritually and to pray faithfully in the knowledge and understanding he has. And if he has no desire to grow spiritually or to invest his gifts, pray for him that his heart will change, that the Holy Spirit will teach and convict him, and that he will ultimately escape the judgment the unfaithful one-talent servant received.

IF THE WALLS ARE THERE, HOW CAN YOU BEGIN TO TEAR THEM DOWN?

PERHAPS THE SPIRITUAL wall of unfulfilled expectations is already in place, cemented well and firmly planted between you and your husband. What now?

First, begin praying within yourself and then aloud:

> *Lord Jesus, I accept my husband the way You accept my husband. I surrender to You all my expectations of him. Change him, Lord. Make him, and me, like You.*
>
> *—Amen*

In summary of the insights from this chapter, decide that you will act upon them by:

▷ *Expecting* the best and not the worst from your husband.
▷ *Speaking* about his successes and refusing to remind him of his failures.
▷ *Praying* for his justification and sanctification in Christ Jesus.
▷ *Surrendering* all your expectations for your husband to Jesus Christ.
▷ *Refusing to take up* the bait of offense.
▷ *Repenting* of your hold upon past offenses and asking your husband's forgiveness for taking up offenses in the past.

Finally, tell yourself the truth. Unfulfilled expectations from the past serve no constructive purpose in the present. They can only serve to continue the hurt, pain, and regrets of the past. Bury them along with your present expectations. Refuse to dig them up again, even when you are angry and want to hurt your husband in an argument or conflict.

Imagine this. Take all your past unfulfilled expectations of your husband, write them on slips of paper or three-by-five cards, and put them in a trash bag. (Even tell your husband what you are doing.) Put the trash sack out to be picked up on garbage day and then watch the garbage truck haul your sack of unfulfilled expectations off to the dump. Never visit the landfill to retrieve your garbage.

Dismantle the wall. Throw away the bricks of unfulfilled expectations. Enjoy the freedom of surrendering all your expectations to Christ, and celebrate the joy that comes when your husband begins to change, grow spiritually, and pray with you—not because of what you did, but because you prayed and waited while Christ changed him!

•••
ASK YOUR HUSBAND TO READ THIS PRAYER ALOUD WITH YOU. EACH OF YOU SHOULD INSERT THE OTHER'S NAME WHEN YOU COME TO EACH PARENTHESIS:
•••

May the LORD bless (name of your spouse) and protect (name of your spouse).

May the LORD smile upon (name of your spouse) and be gracious to (name of your spouse).

May the LORD show (name of your spouse) His favor and give (name of your spouse) His peace. Amen.

—ADAPTED FROM NUMBERS 6:24–26, NLT

If your husband will not pray this prayer aloud with you, then don't give up. Pray it over him. Let him know that you pray blessing and grace over him continually.

Get ready to dismantle the next wall—that of unmet needs. Get a box of tissues. The tears are about to flow. Turn to the next chapter.

Listen, Lord,

    a mother's praying
    low and quiet:
    listen please.

Listen what her tears
    are saying,
    see her heart
    upon its knees;
    lift the load
    from her bowed shoulders
    till she sees
    and understands,

You, who hold
    the worlds together,
    hold her problems
    in Your hands.

—RUTH GRAHAM BELL
20TH CENTURY A.D.

4

Breaking Down the
Spiritual Walls of ...

UNMET NEEDS,
UNPRIZED GIFTS, AND
UNRECOGNIZED SACRIFICES

THE WALL OF UNMET NEEDS

FOR YEARS JENNIFER had hungered for spiritual intimacy with her husband. They had waited for five years to have their first child. John's schooling had come first. Then they had moved to Denver to take a new job, buy their first home, and become established and stable as a couple. Finally, they felt ready to have a child.

Jennifer was looking forward to this birth with more than the normal expectancy. Secretly she hoped that this child would provide her with the spiritual and physical intimacy she had given up hope of ever having with John.

Yes, she and John had prayed occasionally for the health of the coming baby and thanked God for the blessing it would be to have a child. But Jennifer's need for a husband who would lovingly linger with her in prayer and intensely hunger for God's Word was never met. She compared John to other young husbands in their small home group who seemed so eager to grow spiritually. But John was content with his spiritual status quo and never pushed on to a deeper walk with God.

Then tragedy struck. Jennifer began bleeding one morning while John was away on a business trip. A friend rushed her to the nearby hospital emergency room. There, alone with her fears, Jennifer miscarried, losing not only her baby but also the one she had hoped would meet her unmet needs.

Jennifer's friend tried unsuccessfully all afternoon to reach John who was traveling from one meeting to the next. Finally, late that evening and hours after the miscarriage, John and Jennifer talked on the phone.

But her husband was distant—not only geographically but also emotionally. Tritely commenting, "Well, I guess it must just be God's will for us not to have a child now," with a tired voice, John said he had to get some sleep and hung up the phone, unaware that he had just hung up on the relationship as well.

Jennifer grieved privately for her lost child and continued her silent suffering of unmet needs. She needed her husband to pray with her, share spiritually with her, be both her husband and friend, and grow with her in a deeper intimacy with God. John had no desire to meet those needs. Going to church once a week was all he wanted for his spiritual life. His days and nights were filled with work. John believed that he was meeting his wife's needs by providing for her material needs—money, house, food, clothing, and other luxuries that only money could buy.

Love never promises *stuff*. Love promises a *person*. By promising to love one another unconditionally, husbands and wives promise themselves above all else. To one another, they say something like: "Finally, in my commitment of unconditional love I promise you a person, not a piece of putty."[1] We must love people and use things instead of loving things and using people. We may use things to serve people, but we cannot meet people's need for love with things. John believed that working hard and providing Jennifer with stuff met her need for love. Sadly, his belief was heresy, and her needs went unmet.

No amount of money could assuage Jennifer's need for companionship and spiritual partnership. Years of unmet needs had built a wall between her and John. Their marriage had become a business relationship. Even when they went to church, they drove in separate cars, sat in different places, and worshiped in different ways. She overflowed with feeling and emotion as she worshiped while John stoically endured the service, constantly checking his watch to see how much longer he would be stuck in church until lunchtime finally arrived.

Have your unmet needs built a wall of separation between you and your husband? Whenever your husband fails to meet a physical, emotional, intellectual, or spiritual need that you have, how do you respond?

The deepest need we have is to love and be loved. When our love for another is unrequited, something within us cries out in pain and misery. Such was the situation in the ancient days of the patriarchs when Leah harbored a deep need to be loved and cherished by her husband, Jacob. Let's uncover what happened with Leah and her unmet need for love.

LEAH'S UNMET NEED FOR LOVE

THE ANCIENT, SEMITIC marriage rite proceeded along the prescribed customs of the day. The nomadic clan leader Laban had promised his daughter, Rachel, to his nephew, Jacob, in exchange for seven years of hard labor. Willingly and expectantly, Jacob had worked as hard as any slave tending his uncle's flocks until that long-awaited day arrived—the marriage feast.

Well-wishers gathered from far and near to celebrate the marriage feast. Covered from head to toe in luxurious robes and veils, not even the bride's eyes were visible through the translucent veil that covered her face.

Jacob's heart pounded. At long last, he would spend the first night of the rest of his life with the woman he loved. The feast seemed to last forever, but then the night came when Jacob went in to his beloved...only to discover the next morning that the woman he made love to in the night was Leah, not Rachel! Consumed with fury, Jacob accosted Laban, "What is this you have done to me? I served you for Rachel, didn't I? Why have you deceived me?" (Gen. 29:25).

Laban excused his deception, protesting that he must first marry off his older daughter Leah—with the crossed eyes—before her younger sister could marry. So Jacob agreed to work another seven years in order to marry the woman he really loved—Rachel.

So what about Leah? What is she to do? How is she to feel? How will her needs for love be met if her husband disdains her and loves another? God

72

supernaturally intervenes to comfort Leah:

> When the LORD saw that Leah was not loved,
> he opened her womb, but Rachel was barren.
> Leah became pregnant and gave birth to a
> son. She named him Reuben, for she said, "It
> is because the LORD has seen my misery.
> Surely my husband will love me now." She
> conceived again, and when she gave birth to a
> son she said, "Because the LORD heard that I
> am not loved, he gave me this one too." So
> she named him Simeon.
>
> —GENESIS 29:31–33

Even after bearing six sons and one daughter, Leah was still looking for honor, respect, and love from Jacob (Gen. 30:20). Wisely, Leah never let a spiritual wall develop between her and God as she continually gives praise to Him for her children. Upon the birth of Judah, she exclaimed, "This time I will praise the LORD" (Gen. 29:35). And when Zebulun was born, "God has presented me with a precious gift" (Gen. 30:20). Leah's need for love, honor, and respect from her husband, Jacob, goes unmet. Apparently it is only in death that Leah is honored, being buried with the patriarchs—Abraham and Isaac. Later Jacob would give instructions to be buried with Leah, in the place of traditional honor, and not with Rachel, who had been buried at another site (Gen. 49).

It is also interesting to note that nowhere does Scripture report any animosity from Leah toward Jacob. In fact, she and Rachel work together on Jacob's behalf to get their inheritance from Laban.

The Scripture honors Leah and Rachel as two women who "together built the house of Israel" (Ruth 4:11).

If you had been Leah, how would you have responded? Do unmet needs in your marriage cause spiritual walls to go up between you and your husband? Could you have continued to support and cooperate with your husband if you were being treated the way Jacob treated Leah?

AVOIDING THE SPIRITUAL WALL OF UNMET NEEDS

THE LIFE OF LEAH provides a valuable insight into how wives can detour around the temptation to build a spiritual wall between themselves and their husbands when their needs go unmet. The key to breaking down the wall of unmet needs, or to not even building the wall in the first place, is praise!

Early in her marriage, Leah had to face the reality that Jacob would not meet her deep need for love. He clearly loved Rachel. Leah was not his first love or his first choice. She did experience misery and grief, but she got over it. How? She praised God for His goodness and grace in the midst of her unmet needs. Leah thanked God for the precious gift of her children.

In order to elude a spiritual wall resulting from unmet needs, it's essential that you...

▶ *Recognize that God, not your husband, is your source.* God meets your needs. Paul wrote, "And my God will meet all your needs according to his glorious riches in Christ Jesus" (Phil. 4:19). Say this passage aloud several times: "My God will meet all my needs according to His glorious riches in Christ Jesus."

➤ *Praise God for the good gifts He has given you.*
Refuse to focus on your lack. Have an attitude of
gratitude for what God has and will provide.
"And God is able to make all grace abound to
you, so that in all things at all times, having all
that you need, you will abound in every good
work" (2 Cor. 9:8). Remember that all the good
gifts in life do not come as the result of what
your husband does or doesn't do. Every good
and perfect gift comes from just one source—the
Lord. "Every good and perfect gift is from above,
coming down from the Father of the heavenly
lights, who does not change like shifting shadows"
(James 1:17).

➤ *Refuse to build spiritual walls because you do not
get what you want.* Remember that God meets
your *needs,* not your *wants.* Blaming God for not
getting what you want reveals an inner spirit of
complaining and discontent. Again Scripture
gives us the insight we need: "I have learned to
be content whatever the circumstances. I know
what it is to be in need, and I know what it is to
have plenty. I have learned the secret of being
content in any and every situation, whether well
fed or hungry, whether living in plenty or in
want. I can do everything through him [Christ]
who gives me strength" (Phil. 4:11–13).

➤ *Pray and ask for what you need.* First, ask God for
your needs. Whatever is in His will for you, in the
power of His name, that will He do. "And I [Jesus]
will do whatever you ask in my name, so that the
Son may bring glory to the Father. You may ask
me for anything in my name, and I will do it"

(John 14:13–14). Remember that husbands are not mind readers and often have poor intuition for perceiving what their wives need. When you have a need, ask for it. If you need him to pray for or with you, ask him. Don't fear that he will say no. But even as you ask, realize that *he* is not your source, *God* is. If he fails to meet your need, your heavenly Father knows your needs and cares for you. (See Matthew 6:25–34.)

▶ *Repenting of the Wall of Unmet Needs* ◀

Almighty God, I have physical, emotional, mental, and spiritual needs. I repent of the hurt I have felt when my mate could not meet all my needs or even the needs that I desperately wanted him/her to meet.

I know, God, that You are my source, the river of life and healing for every part of my existence. Everything I need is known to You, and You care for me.

I repent of my wants. I have desires in my flesh that I now crucify. I am crucified with Christ. Nevertheless, I live, yet not I, but Christ lives in me.

Help me, Father, to share my needs, and give my mate the ability to meet my every need as he/she is able. Reveal to me the ways You would have me pursue to have my needs met according to Your purposes.

Jesus, my deepest, heartfelt need is You. I love and desire You with all my heart. You are my first love and the passion of my life. Christ, through Your power I pull down the wall of unmet needs and lean on You for everything in life.

—Amen

M

In unison, read aloud the following verses:

Let the LORD's people show him reverence, for those who honor him will have all they need.
—PSALM 34:9, NLT

"My gracious favor is all you need. My power works best in your weakness." So now I am glad to boast about my weaknesses, so that the power of Christ may work through me.
—2 CORINTHIANS 12:9, NLT

The LORD your God has blessed everything you have done and has watched your every step through this great wilderness. During these forty years, the LORD your God has been with you and provided for your every need so that you lacked nothing.
—DEUTERONOMY 2:7, NLT

THE WALL OF UNPRIZED GIFTS

HANK ALWAYS MADE Victoria feel worthless, especially in the area of spiritual authority. He was always the one who had spiritual gifts. He was always the one who had a word from God. He was always the one who did ministry. Victoria's role was to

77

remain quietly in his shadow, supporting everything he said and did, and never questioning his directives or decisions. He called such a relationship *biblical.* She felt as if she had been drafted unwillingly into his navy. He ran his marriage and family like a ship's captain, and anyone who crossed him had to walk the plank!

Reality was that Victoria did have some wonderful and valuable gifts, both in the marriage and in ministry. However, Hank was too caught up in himself and his ministry to notice her gifts or to affirm her. When Victoria finally came in for a counseling session, her self-worth was shattered.

Victoria continually used her gifts of hospitality and administration to keep their home and ministry together. When people called the house to talk to Hank and he was out, Victoria would encourage, comfort, and counsel them very effectively on the phone. Often her counsel was so effective that they never called Hank, because God met their needs through Victoria's giftings.

Hank and Victoria did pray together, but she found that time of prayer very unsatisfying. He would pray for the two of them and never invite her to pray anything. Hank treated his wife as if she had nothing to say, nothing to pray, and nothing to give.

As Christians, we not only have the need to receive, we also have the need to give. And Hank stifled Victoria's need to give. Yet her prayers with others were effective, compassionate, and uplifting. It seemed that everyone knew how spiritually gifted Victoria was except her own husband. Others appreciated her giftings, but he never noticed.

As she shared her frustrations with her husband,

it became apparent that a wall of unrecognized gifts was firmly in place between her and her husband. Her significance was not affirmed by the person who meant the most to her. As a result, when he prayed she didn't listen. When he preached, she mentally redecorated the house. When he gave orders, she responded with passive aggression. She passively refused to respond to his control as a way to get back at him. She was like the child told by her parent to stand in the corner. Outwardly the child was standing, but inwardly she was sitting in rebellion and anger. Outwardly Victoria was a submissive wife, but inwardly she was shutting her husband out of her life.

Failing to recognize the spiritual gifts of a spouse actually quenches the Spirit in that person's life. Paul writes, "Do not put out the Spirit's fire" (1 Thess. 5:19). Putting a damper on the Spirit's fire can cause love to wax cold in the spiritual life of a couple. So if your husband does not appreciate your gifts, you can take some positive steps toward avoiding a wall of unappreciated gifts.

1. *Keep using your gifts.* The source and prompting of your gifts comes from the Holy Spirit, not from your husband (1 Cor. 12). Be obedient to the Spirit in ministering your gifts.
2. *Be Spirit-led.* Don't force your gifts on your husband or anyone else. Listen to the Spirit's voice.
3. *Stay accountable in a spiritual support group.* Having a small group of spiritually mature women with whom you can pray

and minister will encourage you in your gifts and ministry.

4. *Ask for affirmation.* Whenever you operate in the gifts in the company of your husband, ask him for affirmation. How? Simply say, "I was operating in my gift of (name gift). Did you experience God's presence and power?"

5. *Give verbal praise to God for your gifts.* Let your husband hear you give testimony and praise for how His Spirit has ministered to others through you.

▶ *Repenting of the Wall of Unprized Gifts* ◀

Spirit of God, thank You for the talents, skills, and gifts that You have given me. I know they come from You and are to be used to give You glory.

I confess for the times that I have sought glory for using the gifts You have given and for expecting personal recognition of those gifts. I repent for giving with conditions instead of giving unconditionally.

I repent of any pain, anger, or bitterness I have felt toward my mate for not prizing the gifts You have given me. I give You glory for the gifts, talents, and skills that You have used to bless me in his/her life.

Jesus, I cherish the gifts that Your Holy Spirit has deposited in my life, and I now commit myself to using them for the sake of others, not for self-recognition.

In Jesus' name, I remove the wall of

*unprized gifts from my life, understanding
that when I minister Your gift, You will
receive all the glory and honor.
In Jesus' precious name.*

—Amen

ᐳᐸ

In unison with your husband, say aloud these truths:

> Now there are different kinds of spiritual gifts,
> but it is the same Holy Spirit who is the source
> of them all. There are different kinds of service
> in the church, but it is the same Lord we are
> serving. There are different ways God works in
> our lives, but it is the same God who does the
> work through all of us. A spiritual gift is given
> to each of us as a means of helping the entire
> church.
>
> —1 CORINTHIANS 12:4–7, NLT

THE WALL OF UNAPPRECIATED SACRIFICES

AFTER LIVING FOR years in an expensive house in
the city, her husband insisted on moving to a
foreign country. He was uncertain exactly where
they should live in this new country, so he dragged
his family from location to location looking for a
place to settle.

However, nothing seemed to suit him. She moved
continually. She left her family, her family's religious
traditions, her home, her way of life, and her

lifestyle to wander from town to town looking for a new place to live.

Not only was her husband unsettled, he was also demanding. Long after their child-raising years, he wanted to start a family. She just laughed, feeling such desires on his part were preposterous.

The husband was Abraham, and his wife was Sarah. A survey of the narratives in Genesis reveals that while Sarah made tremendous sacrifices and was asked to follow Abraham—who followed an invisible God of whom Sarah had never heard— Abraham rarely showed any appreciation for her. We might protest that his culture treated women like property, and hence he could be excused. But lack of appreciation for sacrifices can never be excused, no matter what culture or time in history.

As the husband who tried to pawn his wife off on Pharaoh to save his own skin, Abraham can never be upheld as a model spouse. In fact, many of the heroes in Scripture were failures as husbands and fathers. Some notable examples of failure were Samuel, Eli, David, and Solomon. Remember that Bathsheba sacrificed her husband, reputation, and simple lifestyle to endure a roller-coaster relationship with David and all his other wives and children—not to mention the court intrigues that sought to kill her and her husband. So, biblical examples of godly husbands were rare. Perhaps Isaac, Joseph, and Boaz might be among the few to qualify as spiritual, servant-leaders in their homes.

Are all men essentially lame when it comes to developing a strong, spiritual walk and prayer life with their wives? Not necessarily, but history gives us few biblical examples of men of God who were also great husbands and fathers. Perhaps the most stellar example is Joseph, the father of Jesus. Yet even he considered hiding Mary away to save face (and probably her life) when he discovered she was pregnant. Did he have no appreciation of the fact that she would have to bear the shame of being an unwed, pregnant mom? So how does one avoid building a wall of unappreciated sacrifices if she is married to an Abraham or a David? Here are a few keys for avoiding the wall of unappreciated sacrifices:

> ▶ *View your sacrifices as gifts.* Never give unwillingly or without joy. Cheerless sacrificial giving transforms sacrifice into duty and involuntary servitude. When Paul asserts that "God loves a cheerful giver," he is not limiting his exhortation to the giving of money, but is indicating giving to any seed that is sown for God's work (2 Cor. 9:6–15). Whatever you sow sacrificially and cheerfully into your husband's life will ultimately reap a harvest of praise and glory to God.

> ▶ *Ask for appreciation when you need it.* Spontaneous appreciation from your husband may be what you really want but may also be a distant reality. If that is the case, then ask now for appreciation and affirmation when you need it. Pray that your husband gets your message and a strong dose of conviction from the Holy Spirit so that he will learn how to appreciate you in the future.

> ▶ *Avoid provoking negative responses from your husband.* Some wives prefer negative responses to no responses. As a result, they stop sacrificing or giving in the hope that their husbands will at least notice and perhaps complain. Heed this

warning: Never seek negative responses as a substitute for edification. God will always affirm you. If your husband refuses to notice, go to your Bridegroom—Jesus.

▶ Repenting of the Wall of Unrecognized Sacrifices ◀

Lord, I know that Your sacrifice on the cross for me overshadows any sacrifice I make in my life for You or in serving others.

I repent for negative feelings or offenses that I have taken up when my mate has not recognized the sacrifices I have made in our marriage.

I ask Your forgiveness and my mate's forgiveness for holding onto negative feelings when recognition did not come my way.

Jesus, Your sacrifice on the cross is everything to and for me. How I long to fellowship in Your sufferings, counting all my achievements and sacrifices as nothing compared to You. Help me to be sensitive and thankful when others make sacrifices for me. Give my mate the ability to notice and affirm the sacrifices I make in our marriage. When he/she notices, fill me with praise for You. And when he/she doesn't notice, fill me still with praise for You. In everything, Jesus, I give You praise.

—Amen

M

In unison, say these verses aloud with your marriage partner:

> As a result, I can really know Christ and experience the mighty power that raised him from the dead. I can learn what it means to suffer with him, sharing in his death, so that, somehow, I can experience the resurrection from the dead! I don't mean to say that I have already achieved these things or that I have already reached perfection! But I keep working toward that day when I will finally be all that Christ Jesus saved me for and wants me to be.
>
> —PHILIPPIANS 3:10–12, NLT

WALLS FROM A HUSBAND'S PERSPECTIVE

JIM AND LILLIAN would never come into the office for counseling, but they did visit with us often over dessert after church. Jim loved to play golf. One afternoon on the back nine, he began to open up about his frustrations with Lillian.

"What do I do with a wife who needs everything all the time?" Jim asked with a sigh.

"What do you mean?" I responded, immediately knowing we were shifting from golf talk to counseling.

"She says I don't meet her needs. She meant emotional and spiritual needs. Sex is okay, I guess," Jim mused.

"What needs does she mention?" I asked.

"She never really gets specific, except she says that I don't pray with the same intensity as she does. She expects me to give her my full attention when I get home from work, but I need some space. When I get home I'm beat, but she has been praying and listening to Christian tapes. She's ready to talk, share, and even pray. All I want is a little space, peace and quiet, and some light entertainment like watching TV or a video."

Lillian was smothering Jim with her needs. And the more he withdrew, the more insistent she became about Jim spending time with her. In fact, Jim was finding reasons to work late, run errands after work, and go to meetings in the evenings just to avoid Lillian. "Nothing gets her off my back," he confessed.

Jim's confessions are similar to those of other husbands who have discovered that the walls of unmet needs, unhealed hurts, and unrepented offenses are increasing the spiritual distance between them and their wives. Here are some of the most common comments I have heard men make:

- ▶ My wife is very demanding. No matter how much I do for or with her, it's never enough.
- ▶ Her emotional tank is on empty every morning, no matter how much we have shared together the day before.
- ▶ If I miss praying with her or reading the Bible with her just one day, it's like everything we've done together before that goes down the tubes.
- ▶ I just can't win. The more I try to meet her needs the more criticized I am.
- ▶ She says I never notice what she does. Am I suppose to notice every time she moves the furniture or changes things around? I like what she does, but I don't like having to notice everything.
- ▶ She cries for no reason at all. She's always

talking about how much she's given up to support me and the kids.

➤ I know she wants to have a ministry at church beyond just being my wife, but I don't know what she wants to do.

➤ Just about the time we settle in on one way to pray and have quiet times together she buys a new book or hears of a new way to share together. I get tired of all her gimmicks.

Almost without fail, men say there are two responses from their wives that they really hate.

1. When a man asks his wife, "What do you need me to pray for?", and receives the answer, "Oh, nothing. I'm just fine," but later receives a lecture about not meeting her needs.

2. When a husband prizes her gifts or appreciates her sacrifice and she responds, "Oh, it was nothing." Such a comment not only puts her down, it also puts down his affirmation.

THE BRIDEGROOM'S PERSPECTIVE

JESUS' LIFE WAS filled with women who had unmet needs, unprized gifts, and unrecognized sacrifice. Mary Magdalene's need for love drove her to prostitution before she met Jesus. The woman at the well had a similar need before drinking of Jesus' living water. Mary and Martha both had special giftings that they used to minister to Jesus. No one in His day but Jesus had befriended and uplifted women like Mary and Martha. And what of Mary, mother of Jesus? She sacrificed everything, even the rebuke of her Son, to be Jesus' mother. Her sacrifice never seems fully appreciated by the disciples and followers of Jesus until perhaps after the resurrection when she is among the one hundred twenty sitting in the room at Pentecost.

Jesus valued, prized, and recognized women. They followed Him and ministered to Him. In turn, Jesus often ministered to woman in unique and nontraditional ways for His era. He transformed man's view of woman from that of property to being a person loved and prized by God. So much did the Bridegroom reach out to meet the needs of women, that stories, miracles, and narratives about Jesus' ministry to women fill the Gospels. Here's a sampling, with observations about each entry:

➤ Jesus' incarnation, birth announcement, and dedication at the temple focus on the faith and obedience of women—Elizabeth, Mary, and Anna the prophetess (Luke 2).

➤ Peter's mother-in-law was gifted in hospitality. When she was sick, Jesus healed her with a touch (Matt. 8:14; Mark 1:29; Luke 4:38).

➤ When the woman with the issue of blood crawled through the crowd to touch the hem of Jesus' cloak, He esteemed her faith saying, "Take heart, daughter, your faith has healed you" (Matt. 9:22; Mark 5:25–34; Luke 8:43–48).

➤ When a Gentile woman who had no right speaking to a Jewish prophet approached Jesus to ask Him to heal her daughter, He not only rebuked her but also saw her heart of faith and honored that faith, saying, "Woman, you have great faith! Your request is granted" (Matt. 15:28; Mark 7:24–29).

‣ Jesus recognized a woman's gifting for worship when she anointed Him with perfume and washed His feet with her tears and hair (Luke 7:38).

‣ Jesus chose to stay in the home of Martha, Mary, and Lazarus when He was close to Jerusalem. He ministered to their needs to worship and serve Him. Jesus prized Mary's worship and taught Martha how to understand the relationship between service and worship (Luke 10:38–41).

‣ Jesus uplifted wives and dignified their position in marriage when He rebuked the Jewish men for finding ways so easily to divorce their wives (Matt. 19:3–12).

‣ In the widow's life, He recognized the gift of giving that far exceeded that of the self-righteous men in the Temple (Mark 12:41–44; Luke 21:1–4).

‣ Jesus broke with Jewish tradition and carried on a solitary conversation with the Samaritan woman. He recognized her need for God and for love. One of the longest spiritual dialogues between Jesus and another person was His ministry with the woman at the well (John 4).

‣ When Lazarus died, Jesus ministered specifically to the need for comfort in the grieving of Martha and Mary and shared profound truths with them about eternal life and resurrection (John 11).

‣ Jesus' first resurrection appearance was not to men but to women (Matt. 28:1–10). And it is to Mary Magdalene—not to the disciples—that He appears in the garden immediately after His

Resurrection. He comforts her in her time of grief (John 20:10–18).

➤ At the time of Pentecost, when the Holy Spirit was sent to baptize and empower the early church, women took their place praying and waiting alongside of men. "They all joined together constantly in prayer, along with the women and Mary the mother of Jesus, and his brothers" (Acts 1:14).

Women were an integral part of Jesus' ministry as well as in the life of the early church. The Bridegroom met the needs of women, prized their gifts, and recognized their sacrifices.

At times, Jesus will be more of a husband to you than the man of flesh that you married. And while your husband may wonderfully meet many of your needs, only the Bridegroom can and will meet all your needs.

Christ has a sensitivity to your needs that no human will ever have. But be encouraged just as David encouraged himself in the Lord (1 Sam. 30:6). Take hope in this: The same Jesus who touched and ministered to women throughout the Gospels indwells born-again husbands so that they have both the power and potential to minister to you as He does. (See 1 Corinthians 3:16–17.)

Pray this:

Jesus, by Your Spirit empower my husband to treat me the way You do, to meet my needs as You do, to prize my gifts as You do, and to recognize my sacrifices as You do.

—Amen

IF THE WALLS ARE THERE,
HOW CAN YOU BEGIN TO TEAR THEM DOWN?

THERE ARE SEVERAL things you can do to begin tearing down the spiritual wall of unmet needs, unprized gifts, or unappreciated sacrifices today:

1. *Spend at least thirty minutes a day with your husband in one-to-one sharing.* No television or distractions. No interruptions allowed. No problem solving, complaining, or criticisms are permitted. You can affirm one another and share real needs for prayer, but you cannot argue, fight, or put one another down. Will you spend thirty, positive, need-meeting minutes with your husband each day?

2. *Make prayer lists for one another of your needs.* Update them regularly as you share with one another. Write down God's answers to your needs. Keep the lists in your Bibles, wallets, or purses. Share with one another the praise for what God is doing in your lives. One way that Judi and I keep scriptures and needs before one another is by writing them on the bathroom mirror with a non-permanent marker. Then whenever I shave or she puts on her makeup, we see the Word and each other's needs, and we pray.

3. *Forgive.* Forgive your husband for not meeting the needs in your life that he can but won't meet. If you cannot speak your forgiveness aloud to your husband, write

91

down your expressions of forgiveness so that he can read your forgiveness over and over again. Ask him to do the same for you—to write down his forgiveness of your offenses against him.

4. *Ask for his forgiveness.* Ask his forgiveness for not meeting the needs you could meet but fail to meet. Sometimes it's easier to forgive than to ask for forgiveness. But when the pain of keeping sin in becomes greater than the fear of exposure, you will confess and ask forgiveness. The Holy Spirit will continue to work in you, convicting you of sin until you repent and confess. (See John 16.)

5. *Become realistic.* No human being can ever meet all of another human being's needs. When they try to do so the relationship becomes dependent or codependent, with one person using or abusing the other. Your spouse cannot meet all your needs for relationship and friendship. Some of your needs will have to be met appropriately by other Christians.

A dear friend of mine, Dr. Marylea Henderson, has counseled women for over three decades through Displaced Homemakers' centers on college campuses. As an adjunct counselor on our church staff, she would often give wise supervision in case conferences we had where we evaluated our counseling experiences. Marylea worked specifically with women who had been displaced through separation, divorce, death, or disability. She had been divorced years earlier from an abusive, alcoholic husband and had never remarried. For decades she listened to and counseled an unending stream of hurting women through the painful crises of their lives.

In one of our supervision sessions, I asked Marylea, "Should a husband and wife meet one another's needs on a 50/50 basis in marriage?"

"No," she quickly retorted, "they should meet at 100/100. In other words, both should seek to meet the other's needs with 100 percent of their abilities."

"Then will it be possible to meet *all* the other person's needs?" I asked.

"Not at all. What a wife needs to know is that her husband is giving his best to her. But his best will never meet all of her needs for meaningful relationships. At best, he may meet half or two-thirds of her needs. She also needs a network of friends who will be there to meet her other needs. A wife should never expect her mate to meet all of her needs."

6. *Find others to pray with you.* Our need to pray with another person will only be met partially by praying with our spouses. We also need Christian friends to pray with us in home groups, prayer meetings, worship services, and over the phone. However, one word of caution at this point: When selecting a prayer partner for one-to-one

praying together, select a partner of the same gender. If a woman selects a male prayer partner who is not her husband, the dangers of transference of feelings arise and could lead to inappropriate or immoral behaviors and emotions.

Joan's husband was quiet and reserved. He would pray silently with her but never aloud. But Joan was in a prayer group at work that involved both men and women.

At times, the prayer group would divide up into pairs and pray for one another. Joan often found herself praying with Jeff, who prayed aloud easily and seemed to know just the right words to pray for her needs. More and more, Joan found herself sharing the intimate needs of her life when she and Jeff prayed together.

After some time passed, they occasionally would eat lunch together and just share about their families and personal concerns. Both had pure motives. Both loved God. But an emotional bond began to develop between them that led them deeper and deeper into an adulterous relationship. Both eventually divorced their mates and married each other.

You may believe that this cannot happen to you. Don't deceive yourself. Anyone can be tempted and can yield to temptation. Refuse to put yourself into a place or relationship that can compromise your relationship with God or your spouse.

Pray the following prayer aloud:

Lord Jesus, thank You for anticipating and meeting my every need. Give me gratitude for the needs my husband does meet and grace for the needs he cannot meet.
—Amen

In summary, the spiritual insights for breaking down the spiritual wall of unmet needs in this chapter are:

➤ Your source is Christ—He alone can meet all your needs.
➤ Surrender your wants, and seek God for your needs.
➤ Ask your husband for what you need, and invite him to share his needs with you.
➤ Give thanks for the needs your husband can meet, and give the unmet ones to the Lord.
➤ Develop a network of Christian friends that you can pray with in home groups, worship, prayer meetings, and over the phone.
➤ Refuse to let your unmet needs become a wall between your husband and you.

Allowing anger or frustrations to fester over unmet needs, unprized gifts, and unrecognized sacrifices can result in bitter walls being formed between you and your husband. In the next chapter, we will describe the walls of unhealed hurts, unresolved anger, and unrepented offenses. Prepare to allow the Healer to bind up your broken heart.

Jesus, whenever I have unmet needs, unprized gifts, or unrecognized sacrifices, fill me with the wisdom to turn to You. Guard my heart and mouth with Your Word. Give me the words to say to my husband so that he will understand my needs. Thank You, Lord, for being my source.

—Amen

Grant, O Lord, that we may carefully watch over our tempers and every unholy feeling; remove whatever in us may be a stumblingblock in another's way; that, by conforming to Your will in small things, we may hope by Your protection and help to pass safely through the greater dangers and trials to which we may be exposed.

—CHRISTINA ROSSETTI
19TH CENTURY A.D.

Breaking Down the
Spiritual Walls of …

UNHEALED HURTS, UNRESOLVED ANGER, AND UNREPENTED OFFENSES

THE WALL OF UNHEALED HURTS

THE HURTS THAT Monica felt were only indirectly related to her husband, Al. He hadn't caused the hurts, but his church had. They had attended the same church for the entire seven years of their marriage. It was his church, with his parents, his relatives, and his traditions.

Monica had been the outsider from the start. She had come from the same type of church background so she felt that she understood Al's church from the start. What she understood was the teaching, worship style, and doctrines. But what she had learned was just how complex and difficult the relationships in a family church could be.

Some of the women had gossiped about her from the very beginning. Her clothes, home, marriage, and later parenting had all come under the scrutiny and criticism of both relatives and other church members. So many hurtful things had been said that

Monica was now simply numb when she went to church. She got nothing out of the worship and desperately held onto her cool until the benediction. Most Sundays she rushed from the service to pick up Joshua and Benjamin from the nursery and then bolted to the car, avoiding contact with as many people as possible. Of course, her avoidance simply served to fuel the gossip.

Al was a deacon in the church and a high-school Sunday school teacher. Everyone told Monica how fortunate she was to have such a godly man for a husband. Everyone felt Al had married beneath his position in life and let Monica know how they felt. The wall of hurts had built to the point that whenever Al wanted to pray with her or have Bible story time with the children Monica felt sick. Anything that reminded her of his church was repulsive to her. Al was also hurt by her response and finally just gave up trying. Both desperately wanted to grow together spiritually, but the wall of church hurts had become impenetrable.

Hurts can arise from many different wounds. In particular, religious wounds can devastate a couple's prayer life together. Hurts arising from legalism, judgmental and critical attitudes, and rigid traditionalism stifle both God's Spirit and prayer.

Of course, emotional and physical hurts also build a spiritual wall between spouses that only the balm of Gilead can heal.

A WOMAN IMPRISONED BY WALLS OF HURT

SHE HAD VAINLY searched for love with six different men and been met with hurt and rejection from five. The man she now lived with had not taken her to be his wife. Was he also hurting her simply by using her?

She had studied religion. She had heard the traditions of her ancestors who had remained behind in Judah after Babylon had exiled the top strata of Jewish society to Mesopotamia. Those left behind to scratch out an existence in a wasted land were the poor, the sick, the crippled, and the outcasts of Jewish society. Out of this human rubble arose a hybrid group of people known as Samaritans. They intermarried with pagans. They tried to worship God in ways different from the Torah because there was no temple, no priesthood, and no sacrifice left in the land.

When Nehemiah refused to let the Samaritans help with the rebuilding of Jerusalem, they held their own religious observances in Samaria. On Mount Gerizim, the Samaritans had built a temple to rival Zerrubbabel's temple, which had been built in Jerusalem when the Jews returned to Jerusalem and rebuilt the walls under Nehemiah. They developed their own priesthood and religious laws in competition with the Jews.

This Samaritan woman had inherited a past filled with religious hurts passed on from generation to generation. She had lived from one hurt to the next, inflicted by a succession of men who had rejected her. Her solitary trek to the well may well have indicated that the other women of the village shunned and ostracized her. Her unhealed hurts left her suspicious and untrusting, dogmatic and skeptical, lonely and dry. But now the dry season of her life was about to end by meeting the One who would reveal the source of living water.

The woman had become a desert. Jesus spoke to her dry and arid spirit this way: "Everyone who drinks this water will be thirsty again, but whoever drinks the water I give him will never thirst. Indeed, the water I give him will become in him a spring of water welling up to eternal life" (John 4:13–14).

Interestingly, the woman responded quickly and desperately, "Sir, give me this water so that I won't get thirsty and have to keep coming here to draw water" (John 4:15).

Revealing her need, the woman is not ready to face the reality of her spiritual wall of unhealed hurts.

Have you ever noticed how often the presenting problems and discussions with a person are never the real, underlying problems? We often think we need to solve one problem when a deeper one is really crying out for a solution.

Such is true with this Samaritan woman. The issue has nothing to do with Samaritans and Jews or ancestry and wells. Rather, the problem lay deep within this woman—her inner well was dry, and her soul was parched, sucked dry by the withering winds of hurt and pain.

Jesus is about to pour a refreshing stream into her life that will expose her hurts and heal her pain.

DISMANTLING THE WALL OF UNHEALED HURTS

JESUS HELPED THE Samaritan woman to dismantle her wall of unhealed hurts with truth and compassion— by speaking the truth in love. The Great Physician treated her unhealed hurts by...

1. *Confronting the pain.* Before a hurt can be healed, the pain must be recognized and admitted.
2. *Facing reality.* Denial often leaves our hurts untouched and therefore unhealed. We cannot run from the truth.
3. *Describing the hurt.* Jesus accurately describes the situations in which the woman was hurt.

Prayer is an effective tool used by God's Spirit to help us heal. Just as the Samaritan woman conversed with Jesus and dealt with her unhealed hurts, so we can commune with Him and pray through our pain. How? Go to the healing Word of God.

Read through the Psalms. Highlight all the places that speak of God's comfort, healing, and forgiveness. Underline every place that talks about affliction, hurt, and pain. Then daily read at least one passage about affliction and one about healing, knowing that God understands your hurt and desires to heal and restore you.

Husbands and wives can begin to tear down the spiritual wall of unhealed hurts by first identifying the pain that resides deep within their seared memories of hurtful events. Then they can go to Scripture to uncover the healing balm of God's Word and Spirit for their lives.

Jesus' reality check for the Samaritan woman was His statement, "Go, call your husband and come back" (John 4:16).

He saw through her religious questions and defensiveness to the real pain beneath the surface. He confronted the cause of her pain—rejection. Walls of emotional hurt rise up quickly from the bricks of rejection. Spouses experience rejection from one another in a multitude of ways. But regardless of the reasons or the circumstances, *rejection* often puts a spiritual wall between spouses.

Another brick in the wall of unhealed hurts is *invasion,* which occurs when a spouse invades the boundaries of the other spouse. For example, a husband insists on his own way and bulldozes over his wife's feelings, thoughts, opinions, and wishes. In reflecting on this kind of hurt, Gary Smalley advises, "Ask for permission to enter someone else's space."[1] When a spouse violates 1 Corinthians 13:5 and insists on his or her own way, then hurts result and spiritual walls are erected.

A spiritual wall of unhealed hurts may also be caused by *indifference, inattention, or neglect.* A wife may discern that her husband is indifferent to her physical, emotional, or spiritual needs. She may desire to pray or seek God, but he shows no interest whatsoever in her spiritual desires. He fails to give any attention, worth, or to even listen to her when spiritual matters are discussed. And he neglects even the simple disciplines of saying grace at a meal or attending worship services with her. Having been hurt spiritually early in a marriage, a wife may then withdraw, never again attempting to seek God with her husband.

Finally, *legalism* can construct an almost impenetrable spiritual wall between spouses. If either husband or wife has a strict legalistic religion that jumps to judge and withholds forgiveness, the spouse who breaks the rules is bound to get blasted by the legalistic one. The critical, judgmental blast spiritually wounds the one violating the rules. As a result, the legalistic spouse often reminds the guilty one of their weaknesses and failures without ever forgiving, affirming, or edifying the other. Such legalism demolishes the spiritual significance of the one being constantly accused. We must be careful not to play into the hands of the accuser. We are not God, and thus not judge or lawgiver. Jesus sternly admonishes us, "Do not judge, or you too will be judged" (Matt. 7:1). Paul encourages us by affirming, "Therefore, there is now no condemnation for those who are in Christ Jesus" (Rom. 8:1).

Whatever the cause of the spiritual barrier of unhealed hurts, the balm of healing comes through Christ's example in John 4 with the Samaritan woman. He not only helps her identify her pain but also tells her how to find healing, living waters. You can follow His model by first praying through the dismantling of your own hurts, and then by praying the same prayers in your husband's hearing.

▶ *Confront the pain.*
▶ *Face reality.*
▶ *Describe the hurt.*

Once the hurt has been admitted, you are now ready to repent and forgive. Repentance and confession mean that you let go of the past hurt and refuse to continue in the pain. Jesus takes your pain upon Himself at the cross. "Surely he took up our infirmities [hurts and diseases] and carried our sorrows, yet we considered him [Christ] stricken by God, smitten by him, and afflicted" (Isa. 53:4). Taking our pain upon Himself when we give it to Him in repentance and

105

confession, Jesus heals us, ". . . and by his wounds we are healed" (Isa. 53:5).

▶ Repenting of the Wall of Unhealed Hurts ◀

Lord, my mate has hurt me. Heal my hurts. Mend my broken heart. Release me from all unhealed hurts from my past. Erase their memory from my mind and their pain from my heart.

I ask You to forgive me of any hurt that I have caused my spouse. I ask his/her forgiveness as well.

Lord Jesus, I bind my emotional, physical, mental, and spiritual hurts to the balm of Gilead, and I receive all the release of Your healing. I put my hurt, pain, grief, regrets, and brokenness at the foot of the cross and receive healing, for by Your stripes I am healed.

By Your stripes my mate is healed. By Your stripes our marriage is healed. I declare that the wall of unhealed hurts is washed away by the blood of Jesus Christ.

—Amen

M

Declare aloud these verses as a couple:

He [God] spoke, and they were healed—snatched from the door of death.

—PSALM 107:20, NLT

Think of it—the LORD has healed me! I will sing his praises with instruments every day of my life in the Temple of the LORD.

—ISAIAH 38:20, NLT

But he was wounded and crushed for our sins. He was beaten that we might have peace. He was whipped, and we were healed!

—ISAIAH 53:5, NLT

He personally carried away our sins in his own body on the cross so we can be dead to sin and live for what is right. You have been healed by his wounds!

—1 PETER 2:24, NLT

TEARING DOWN THE WALL OF UNRESOLVED ANGER

TIME AND AGAIN Bill had promised Tommie that he would change. He promised to pray and have a quiet time with her. He also promised to become more involved in ministering with Tommie in the home group and in the couples' ministry at church.

For a while, Bill would proceed full steam ahead with his promises. But after a few months, he would slide back into old ways and patterns. In a counseling session, Tommie shared her frustrations.

"Bill is always promising a deeper commitment to the Lord and more involvement in serving Christ, but he continually breaks his promise. And then, after we've committed to a ministry at church, I find myself making excuses for why he isn't there. It's very embarrassing, and I'm tired of it," Tommie confided.

Bill shared his perspective, "I want to please Tommie, but I get involved in other things and lose interest in the church stuff. Besides, I feel much more comfortable doing things one-on-one with other couples and not in groups. I don't like sharing about our problems and listening to theirs."

Bill's pattern of trying to please Tommie by making promises to change and then breaking his commitment weeks or months later had been a constant source of hurt for years. This pattern wasn't just with spiritual matters but also in other areas of their marriage. Disappointment after disappointment had resulted in a growing anger within Tommie that never was resolved. Continual hurts that repeat themselves build a wall of unresolved hurt in a couple's spiritual life. Especially painful is when a husband goes through repeated times of repentance, making promises to change, but then he lapses back into old habits and hurtful ways. By the time I counseled with Bill and Tommie, he had given up trying to please her, and her repeated, unhealed hurts had fostered not just unresolved anger but a tempest of volcanic rage within her. Gary Smalley observes:

> This destroyer is *forgotten, unresolved anger*—not just the kind that gnaws at one's stomach night after night but also the type that quietly disappears. At least I used to think it disappeared. But when we bury anger inside us... *it's always buried alive!* Then, when we aren't even aware of its presence, it does its damage, destroying like rust on a car, like moths in a dark closet.[2]

Unhealed hurts leading to unresolved anger may be the most difficult walls and barriers to remove in a spiritual life between spouses. Often, even when the hurts have been healed, the anger still lingers like a cough that persists for weeks after the flu has passed.

The spiritual danger of unresolved anger is that it makes the spouse the enemy. A wife angry with her husband is tempted to pray against him instead of for him. And even if they pray together, her focus on the Lord is distracted by her anger for her husband. While he prays stained-glass prayers that are lovely and beautiful, she feels like throwing rocks through the windows and shattering his holy demeanor. *How dare you pray so piously when you have hurt me so deeply and when I am so angry with you!* she thinks, as he, unaware of the anger, prays on.

After praying together, an angry wife may often make a bitter, biting comment that completely shocks her husband. As a result, he silently resolves to avoid praying with his wife in the future if that's the way she is going to respond. Because the anger has been buried, she doesn't know why she is angry, only that she is. And he doesn't know what he's done wrong, only that he is treated more like an enemy than a friend. So the husband simply withdraws more and more from doing anything spiritually intimate with his angry wife.

Do you have unresolved anger in your marriage relationship? If you have a wall of anger, how does that wall of unresolved anger get pulled down and destroyed?

There are some specific steps that can be taken

by a wife who has stored up unresolved anger because her mate has not repented of the offenses he has committed against her. By following these steps, she can begin to tear down two walls—the wall of unresolved anger *and* the wall of unrepented offenses.

STEPS TO DEAL WITH ANGER

1. *Confess the anger.* God's Word promises: "If we confess our sins, he is faithful and just and will forgive us our sins and purify us from all unrighteousness" (1 John 1:9). The problem with unresolved anger is not what happened in the past—that cannot be changed—but what you will do with that anger now. You can continue to let it fester and become a wall of bitterness that stifles all prayer between you and your husband. Or, you can confess the anger to God and receive healing forgiveness.
2. *Tell your husband what you have confessed.* Let your husband know that the wall of your unresolved anger has been destroyed by the blood of Christ—"and the blood of Jesus, His Son, purifies us from every sin" (1 John 1:7).

   Do not expect a response from your husband. If he responds negatively, refuse to pick up an offense. If he responds positively to your confession, praise the Lord. And if he responds indifferently, don't be discouraged. Release the anger, and go

forward in your relationship with the Lord
and your husband.

3. *Forgive your husband even if he doesn't repent.* Your confession does not guarantee
your husband's repentance. Forgiveness is
initiated with no evidence of repentance
from the offender. Those who crucified
Christ did not ask His forgiveness, but
Jesus forgave them even before they
asked. We are to follow His example.

4. *Live in grace, not law.* The Samaritan
woman felt she had all the rules down
pat. However, what she thought was right
was merely the traditions of men, not the
righteousness of God. Jesus refused to
accept her legalism and offered her the
grace of His living waters. Are you
willing to extend the same grace to your
husband that God has extended to you?

▶ *Repenting of the Wall of Unresolved Anger* ◀

*Burning within me, Lord, has been anger
on which the sun has set and that I have
nursed to a raging fire within me. Forgive
me, Jesus, for being angry and bitter with
my mate.*

*Pull out the root of bitterness from my
hate. Transform my anger into unconditional love for my mate. I repent of hostility
and of all the times I brought up past hurt.
I ask my mate to forgive me as well as
seeking God's forgiveness.*

Father God, I thank You for sparing me

from Your wrath through the blood of Jesus. You have forgiven my iniquities and healed my diseases. You have put my sins as far away as the east is from the west. So I exalt You, Lord, for not executing Your judgment but extending Your mercy through the cross of Christ.

Teach me to be merciful in the same way You show me mercy. Teach me to be quick to listen, slow to anger, and slow to speak.

In Jesus' name, flush away my wall of unresolved anger with Your forgiveness, love, and reconciliation. Lord, Your mercies are new every morning.

—Amen

М

Read this passage together:

And "don't sin by letting anger gain control over you." Don't let the sun go down while you are still angry, for anger gives a mighty foothold to the Devil.

—EPHESIANS 4:26–27, NLT

FORGIVE BEFORE HE REPENTS—DEMOLISHING THE WALL OF UNREPENTED OFFENSES

FORGIVENESS BREAKS DOWN the spiritual wall of unresolved anger and unrepented offenses. If forgiveness must wait for repentance, it may never come. In a marriage, withholding forgiveness until repentance occurs grows a putrid cesspool of anger, hurt, depression, and bitterness.

In fact, unresolved anger grows a root of bitterness. Hebrews warns, "See to it that no one misses the grace of God and that no bitter root grows up to cause trouble and defile many" (12:15).

Go back to the steps given on pages 110 and 111 showing you how to deal with anger. Prayerfully go through these steps again, asking God to complete the work of destroying the wall of unrepented offenses.

You may need to write down your anger and to share what you have written with your husband if you cannot share verbally. Or better yet, why not ask your husband to pray with you when you confess? Let him hear your prayer of confession aloud.

Pray . . .

> *Lord, I confess my unresolved anger because of my mate's unrepented offenses against me. Thank You for forgiving me and dying for my sins even before I asked for Your forgiveness. Uproot any bitterness in my life. Thank You for my purification and cleansing through Your blood.*
>
> *—Amen*

❯ Repenting of the Wall of Unrepented Offenses ❮

> *Lord, I repent of taking up offenses. I have yielded to Satan's bait, and I have harbored offenses that have walled me off from You and from my mate.*
>
> *Shatter my offenses, Lord, with Your*

pardon and love. Give me the courage to repent even before my mate repents. Help me to ask him/her to forgive me for taking up an offense.

When my mate does not repent for a wrong, give me the words to express the truth in love without being judgmental, critical, or condemning.

Jesus, You alone are righteous. I confess my pride and arrogance in thinking I have the right to be offended. I surrender all my rights to You and receive the only right I have—to build up and not tear down.

Lion of Judah, crush my wall of unrepented offenses, and teach me to forgive before others repent.

—Amen

M

Read aloud these verses with your spouse:

Please forgive me if I have offended in any way. The LORD will surely reward you with a lasting dynasty, for you are fighting the LORD's battles. And you have not done wrong throughout your entire life. Even when you are chased by those who seek your life, you are safe in the care of the LORD your God, secure in his treasure pouch! But the lives of your enemies will disappear like stones shot from a sling!

—1 SAMUEL 25:28–29, NLT

And tell him:

"God blesses those who are not offended by me [Jesus]."

—MATTHEW 11:6, NLT

A HUSBAND'S PERSPECTIVE

WHAT IS THE view like from a husband's side of a wall of unhealed hurts, unresolved anger, and unrepented offenses? The wall may be partially of his construction. Whatever he has built, he is responsible to break down through the power of Christ.

As husbands experience the walls of hurt and anger built by their wives, they have some specific responses. Here are some of the things I have heard husbands say in countless counseling sessions and small groups. Your husband may be thinking, observing, or even saying some of these things:

- What good will it do if I repent? She'll just find something else to be angry about.
- I can't do anything right, so why try?
- Just stay out of her way, and she'll get over it.
- Every time we try to talk, she just cries, and I feel like a beast.
- I can't heal her hurts and don't know who can.
- My wife sets all the spiritual rules in our family. If I don't live up to her laws, then I'm constantly judged as being unspiritual and even condemned as a lousy spiritual leader in our family.
- The more I try the worse it gets.
- When I have tried to forgive in the past it works for a while, but then something sets her off and she brings up all the hurt again. I'm tired of trying, and I'm tired of listening to her hurt.

115

- When I ask her what I have done, she says that if I really loved her I would know.
- When I try to pray with her, she calls me a hypocrite.
- Her anger makes me angry, so we both just end up shouting at each other and hurting each other more. At least when we don't talk or pray together, we don't hurt each other.
- I'm hurting and angry, but I cannot tell her. We are just overwhelmed.
- The hurts are so many and so deep they will never heal.

You cannot change the way your husband thinks or feels, but you can pray for Christ to change him. And you can change your responses to your husband. Confess this: "I can do everything through him [Christ] who gives me strength" (Phil. 4:13).

At first, any change you make will feel awkward and risky. When you have been hurt and now are healing, he may still treat you like a patient. Act like a victor, not a victim. Do not let his reactions change your direction toward healing. Your responses are to the Bridegroom, not to your groom. Remember, whatever you do, do it unto the Lord (Rom. 14:8).

Your selfless, righteous words and actions will affect your husband in one significant way: They will bring truth and conviction into his life. He may accuse you of being self-righteous, super-spiritual, overly pious or a Jesus freak. Again, don't react to him...don't defend yourself...and don't get offended. Keep your focus on Christ. In fact, His Spirit may use you as a humble vessel to bring your husband to repentance.

THE BRIDEGROOM'S PERSPECTIVE

"HE [THE FATHER] sent forth his word [Jesus the Christ, the Bridegroom] and healed them" (Ps. 107:20). Your husband cannot heal your hurts; neither can you, your friends, your pastor, your counselor, or any other person. Only God, *Jehovah-Rapha,* can heal your hurts and repair the damage caused by unrepented offenses and unresolved anger. Hear God's voice, "I will not bring on you any of the diseases I brought on the Egyptians, for I am the Lord who heals you" (Exod. 15:26).

Egypt—that's the past, the place of slavery and bondage where you were hurt. Don't go back to Egypt! In Egypt the children of God were slaves building tombs, walls of death. Stop returning to the past hurts, offenses, and anger. The Word has healed you and set you free: "Then you will know the truth, and the truth will set you free" (John 8:32). Jesus is the Word sent forth to heal you and set you free. You will never be free to pray with your husband until you are first free to pray with the Bridegroom. The way to approach your husband with forgiveness is through Christ. He empowers you to heal, to forgive, and to pray for and with your husband.

To your anger, the Bridegroom says, "But I tell you that anyone who is angry with his brother [or spouse] will be subject to judgment...Therefore, if you are offering your gift at the altar and there remember that your brother [or spouse] has something against you, leave your gift there in front of the altar. First go and be reconciled to your brother; then come and offer your gift" (Matt. 5:22–24).

About offenses, Jesus observed, "It is impossible

117

but that offences will come" (Luke 17:1, KJV). Others will do sinful, hurtful, and offending things to you—including your husband. The key is not to take the bait of Satan and become offended. The spiritual walls that you erect as a result of offenses and hurts will not protect you! They will only become a barrier between you and the Lord and between you and your husband. God's Word reminds us, "A brother [or spouse] offended is harder to be won than a strong city: and their contentions are like the bars of a castle" (Prov. 18:19, KJV).

We construct walls when we are hurt to safeguard our hearts and prevent any future wounds. We guard our rights and personal relationships carefully. Our energy is consumed with making sure no future injuries will occur. If we don't risk being hurt, we cannot give unconditional love. Unconditional love gives others the right to hurt us. Love does not seek its own, but hurt people become more and more self-seeking and self-contained. In this climate the love of God waxes cold.[3]

Unhealed hurts stifle prayer between you and your husband. Beyond that, they cause your love to wax cold for both God and your husband. About forgiveness, Jesus—your Bridegroom and eternal husband—says to you, "For if you forgive men when they sin against you, your heavenly Father will also forgive you" (Matt. 6:14). Forgiveness destroys the walls and releases you to heal, forgive, and love.

Finally, Jesus confirms that we live by grace, not by law. He teaches us that we must avoid judging others (Matt. 7:1–6) and that true fulfillment of the law is found not in our good works but in Him (Matt. 5:17). Your Bridegroom is perfect, but your groom stands strong only when he is continually gripped by grace.

In summary, the spiritual insights in this chapter for breaking down the spiritual walls of unhealed hurts, unresolved anger, and unrepented offenses are:

➤ Your healer is Christ—He alone can heal your hurts.

➤ To tear down the spiritual wall of unhealed hurts, you must confront the pain, face the reality, and describe the hurt.

➤ Release the offender and forgive him.

➤ Confess your anger to God and to your husband either verbally or in writing.

➤ Forgive your husband whether he repents or not.

➤ Don't go back to unrepented offenses or unresolved anger. Let it go so that you can go forward with God.

➤ Begin praying the Lord's prayer over your husband.

• •

NOW WE CAN TURN TO A FINAL SET OF SPIRITUAL WALLS THAT HINDER OUR PRAYERS AND SPIRITUAL INTIMACY IN MARRIAGE. THESE ARE THE WALLS OF UNCONFESSED SIN, UNDIGNIFIED COMMUNICATION, AND UNFEELING RESPONSES. LEAVE EGYPT AND YOUR SLAVERY TO HURTS BEHIND AND MOVE AHEAD WITH GOD TO WALL-LESS FREEDOM AND LIBERTY IN CHRIST.

• •

Jesus, You are my healer—heal our marriage and keep us healthy, whole, and one in You. Help me to forgive others as You have forgiven me. I forgive my spouse. I repent of any past offenses I have held onto, in Jesus' name.

—Amen

We thank Thee with all our hearts for every gracious dispensation, for all the blessings that have attended our lives, for every hour of safety, health, and peace, of domestic comfort and innocent enjoyment. We feel that we have been blessed far beyond any thing that we have deserved; and though we cannot but pray for a continuance of all these mercies, we acknowledge our unworthiness of them and implore Thee to pardon the presumption of our desires.

Keep us, O Heavenly Father, from evil this night. Bring us in safety to the beginning of another day and grant that we may rise again with every serious and religious feeling which now directs us.

May Thy mercy be extended over all mankind, bringing the ignorant to the knowledge of Thy truth, awakening the impenitent, touching the hardened. Look with compassion upon the afflicted of every condition, assuage the pangs of disease, comfort the broken in spirit.

—JANE AUSTEN
17TH–18TH CENTURY A.D.*

---

*The Book of Uncommon Prayer, edited by Constance and Daniel Pollock (Dallas, TX: Word Publishing, 1996), 9.

Breaking Down the
Spiritual Walls of ...

UNCONFESSED SIN,
UNDIGNIFIED COMMUNICATION,
AND UNFEELING RESPONSES

THE WALL OF UNCONFESSED SIN

SHARON BEGAN WEEPING even before the first word came out. Her sobs shook her shoulders like waves pounding a beach during a summer squall. Finally the storm subsided, and she pulled out each word with painful deliberation.

"I have ruined my marriage," she confided.

My initial response was shock. Sharon and Lance were a model marriage for our young couples. They loved one another and God deeply. They treated each other with the highest respect and love. Often they spoke of their sadness at not being able to have children, and they worked often in the nursery or preschool as volunteers to meet some of their needs for contact with children.

"You have ruined your marriage?" I probed.

"Yes, I told Lance the truth and now everything is ruined."

I didn't really know what she was talking about,

so I simply waited to hear her next revelation.

"You see," she explained, "I had told Lance that I was a virgin when we dated. But that was a lie. And beyond not being a virgin, I had an abortion when I was sixteen. No one knew, not even my parents."

"How does this affect you and Lance?" I asked.

"Last night, I couldn't keep the guilt inside any longer. I had to tell him. I think the abortion I had caused some physical problems that may prevent me from ever having children. So I had to tell Lance the truth. I've never seen him act like he did last night. He was so angry. He said I had deceived him and that he should never have married me. I don't know what to do or where to turn. I'm afraid that Lance will leave me."

Sharon had felt that confession would make things better for her in the marriage. Instead, just the opposite had happened, and now she regretted ever being truthful with Lance. Sometimes the truth in marriage makes things worse before they get better.

Unknown to Lance, all that Sharon had shared with him spiritually had been on a superficial level because she had hidden from him her sin.

• • • • • • • • • • • • • • • •

Robert was a traveling manufacturer's representative. He spent Tuesday through Friday each week on the road calling on the accounts in his region. Living on the road was lonely and boring. Each night he would retreat to his motel room and take refuge in the TV set with its offerings of x-rated movies. Pornography had become his substitute for intimacy.

He never told his wife, Heather, and continued to be a church deacon and a loving father and husband. But Heather sensed that something was not right in their relationship. Whenever Heather suggested that they pray together, he would pray with her but completely avoid any confession of sin or dealing with guilt.

In his *Five Spiritual Vows,* A. W. Tozer instructs Christians to make five vows:

> Deal thoroughly with sin.
> Never own anything.
> Never accept glory.
> Never pass on anything about anyone else that will hurt them.
> Never defend yourself.[1]

Whenever Heather and Robert would talk about confessing sin, he would become defensive and try to change the subject, so Heather never really pushed in this area. Nonetheless, she felt uneasy about his closed silence in this area of their relationship. And from time to time, he made suggestions in their sexual intimacy that sounded strange.

One evening as they were intimate together she pulled away and confronted him. "Is there something going on when you travel that you haven't told me? Are you having an affair?"

Robert froze like a deer caught in the middle of a road by approaching headlights that split the curtain of night, exposing everything by light. He had no place to run or hide.

As they later shared with me their angry fight, which ended in Robert's sleeping on the couch, not only their pretense of spiritual sharing had been shattered but the very viability of the marriage was in jeopardy.

Months of counseling were required to tear down walls that had been built by Robert's unconfessed sin. Before proceeding to examine this wall, let's first make a distinction between real and neurotic guilt. Real guilt arises when we transgress the laws of God, and, as a result, we hurt God, others, or ourselves.

We are destructive. We hurt God: "I have been hurt by their adulterous hearts which turned away from Me" (Ezek. 6:9, NAS). We hurt each other: "Their mouths are full of cursing and bitterness. Their feet are swift to shed blood; ruin and misery mark their ways" (Rom 3:14–16). We constantly cause pain to those we love. Godly remorse seeks to heal, to make restitution to those we've hurt. To the contrary, guilt seeks self-justification. It attempts to get rid of the bad feelings.[2]

Guilt feelings arise when we hurt others. But they may also arise from irrational "shoulds" in our lives that are rooted in unrealistic expectations of ourselves. These "shoulds" create neurotic guilt. We may believe that we should...

> Always have a perfectly clean home.
> Always be ready for unexpected company.
> Always be dressed immaculately for others.
> Always make the right decisions.

When we fail to live up to these unrealistic expectations, we feel guilty. We beat ourselves with guilt that never has to be there. First, examine if your feelings of guilt are real or neurotic. Then proceed to deal with real guilt only while letting go of false, neurotic guilt.

A COUPLE WHOSE GUILT DESTROYED THEM

HOW EXCITED THEY had been to hear the followers of Yeshua proclaiming good news in the temple daily. So many new converts had remained in Jerusalem that the believers who lived there were making room in their homes to house the new family members.

They had heard Yohannan give his testimony.* For years they had seen him sitting at the temple gate begging for any spare coins a passerby might have to give him. Suddenly, one day as the apostles Peter and John were entering the temple they healed the crippled beggar. Yohannan had told everyone about his healing in the name of Yeshua.

Ananias and Sapphira were thrilled by the miracles, signs, and wonders being done in the name of Yeshua. They were especially excited when different believers sold their land and put the money from the sales at the feet of the apostles. The Levite Joseph, whom everyone called Barnabas, had sold a field and given the money for the needy. So Ananias and Sapphira talked between themselves about selling a piece of their property and giving the money to God.

However, their field was the only real asset they owned. *What would happen years from now when they were old?* they thought. They had no children to look after them. Surely they couldn't expect others to

*Fictional name given to the lame man at the temple

127

take care of them. So they decided to keep just a portion back as a nest egg for the future—just in case they needed it in their old age. It seemed innocent and rational enough. Besides, the lion's share of the proceeds was being given to the church. But they wanted the church to think that they had given everything to the Lord, so they secretly plotted a deception in their hearts that could only backfire in tragedy.

Deep inside both knew that what they were doing was deceitful and wrong. But they so wanted to appear supportive and involved in all that the believers were doing. Others would notice what they did and would be impressed with their faith. They didn't even take time to pray about the matter. As soon as Ananias got the money from the sale, he took a portion immediately to the large room where Peter often preached.

Pushing through the crowd listening to Peter, Ananias made his way to the front of the crowd. As Peter preached, Ananias fell to his knees and laid his gift at Peter's feet.

As he stood to walk away, Peter spoke sternly, "Ananias, how is it that Satan has so filled your heart that you have lied to the Holy Spirit and have kept for yourself some of the money you received for the land? Didn't it belong to you before it was sold? And after it was sold, wasn't the money at your disposal? What made you think of doing such a thing? You have not lied to men but to God" (Acts 5:3–4).

Fear seized Ananias' heart. His sin had been exposed. Suddenly, he dropped dead to the ground.

Three hours after some men carried Ananias' body away, Sapphira entered the group of assembled believers in the large meeting room. She was expecting those who knew her to be praising her for the generous gift Ananias had brought earlier to the assembly. Instead, silence greeted her as she made her way through the crowd. Troubled expressions were on the faces of all her friends. Within her stirred the guilt of her sin.

Peter's voice jolted her, "Tell me, is this the price you and Ananias got for the land?" (v. 7). Peter opened his hands and showed the gold pieces he had received from Ananias.

"Yes, that is the price," lied Sapphira (v. 7).

"How could you agree to test the Spirit of the Lord? Look! The feet of the men who buried your husband are at the door, and they will carry you out also" (Acts 5:9). Immediately she dropped dead (v.10).

A wall of unconfessed sin can separate a husband and wife, and it can also separate a couple from God. Let's discover how to tear down the wall of unconfessed sin that builds up in hearts that are hardening toward God.

TEARING DOWN THE WALL OF UNCONFESSED SIN

RHONDA AND TIM sat facing me in the pastor's study. They were a dynamic couple at church. They taught a children's Sunday school class, and she sang in the choir. She complained about his rigid, legalistic approach to faith and his chauvinistic attitudes. It was west Texas, and many men there felt that women were to be silent, "kept" display models—not active, participating mates in marriage and in church leadership. Tim was one of those rugged, west Texas men who appeared very uneasy and embarrassed to be talking with a pastor about his private life.

Tim acknowledged his good-ole-boy ways of handling marriage and life itself. However, he felt that Rhonda wasn't being honest with him about her feelings for him. He did try to share with her spiritually, but she never wanted to pray with him or to read Scripture aloud. She always insisted that their prayer and devotional time be shared as a whole family—never as a couple. After years of trying, Tim had given up trying to be spiritually intimate with Rhonda.

As counseling proceeded, I learned that their physical intimacy was also negligible. As she talked about her career goals and his lack of support, my mind searched for clues beneath the surface of her comments. There was a coldness in her tone of voice toward him that indicated deeper problems in the relationship.

After a number of sessions with both partners, she confided, "I haven't loved Tim for years. I have had men outside of marriage who met my needs, but I know it's wrong. I'm ashamed of my behavior, but two of my girlfriends feel the same way I do. So, we find love outside of marriage. If we take care of our children and husbands, then surely God can't blame us for needing intimacy and love from a kind man who will meet our needs?"

Her adultery had built a wall of unconfessed sin between them that blocked all prayer and spiritual discipline. She had rationalized her sin. Later in the counseling process, she confessed her infidelity to Tim. He reacted angrily at first but then took, as he put it, "a realistic approach" to the problem: "If that's what she needs, and she takes care of the children, house, and my physical needs, then what can I do? At least we can stay together for the sake of the children," Tim reasoned.

Of course, the wall of unrepented sin continued to erode their marriage until, a few years later, they divorced and continued to hurt one another over child-custody issues for years.

The first step toward tearing down a wall of unconfessed sin is confession and repentance. Paul writes, "Godly sorrow brings repentance that leads to salvation and leaves no regret, but worldly sorrow brings death. See what this godly sorrow has produced in you: what earnestness, what eagerness to clear yourselves, what indignation, what alarm, what longing, what concern, what readiness to see justice done. At every point you have proved yourselves to be innocent in this matter" (2 Cor. 7:10–11).

What Rhonda was unable to do was to repent—to turn away from her sinful actions and move toward righteousness in the power of Christ. She admitted that what she was doing was wrong, but she was unwilling to stop it. One counselor shared his basic theory of dealing thoroughly with sin as being:

➤ Admit it.
➤ Quit it.
➤ Forget it.

As simplistic as that may sound, deep truth resides in these tough words.

Deep, spiritual sharing in prayer cannot happen with habitual, unconfessed sin in the life of either partner. Sexual immorality, addiction, abuse, and any involvement with the occult will bring death to a couple's spiritual life together.

What does a wife do when she discerns that un-confessed sin in her husband's life is blocking their intimacy with the Lord as a couple?

The first step is prayer. She needs clear direction from the Lord on how to approach her husband. The Holy Spirit may reveal his sin to her. He may direct her to the Word for strength, insight, and sup-port. At times, the Holy Spirit will bring about circumstances that will reveal the sin. Or, the Spirit may lead them both to counseling. The promise is that God will act when you pray: "Ask and it will be given to you; seek and you will find; knock and the door will be opened to you. For everyone who asks receives; he who seeks finds; and to him who knocks, the door will be opened" (Matt. 7:7–8). Be certain that unconfessed sin will surface. God warns, "And you may be sure that your sin will find you out" (Num. 32:23).

How do you pray? Pray like this:

> *Lord Jesus, I ask that You send Your Holy Spirit to reveal to me and to my mate the wall of unconfessed sin between us. Use the sword of Your Spirit, Your Word, to surgically expose our sin and to remove sin's cancer from our lives. Grant us the courage to confess, the power to repent and walk away from sin, and the freedom we desire to be freed from sin's bondage. Also grant us the love to forgive and the wisdom to forget.*
>
> *—Amen*

Admit it and quit it. Once the sin causing the wall has been revealed, it is important that two actions be taken—admit it and quit it. A wall of unconfessed sin may be built by husband, wife, or both. Whoever is involved in building the wall must not only admit the sin but also quit the sin. If the sin involves addictive behavior or attitudes, both spouses may need counseling in order to break the bondage of sin. Go to a pastor or Christian counselor to start on your pathway toward healing.

Avoid self-deception. Admitting sin takes courage, faith, and determination. Denial and self-deception erode one's willingness to admit sin. Neil T. Anderson and Dave Park have a checklist in *Busting Free* that helps us identify ways we deceive ourselves. Use this checklist yourself or together with your spouse.

WAYS YOU CAN DECEIVE YOURSELF

▶ Hearing God's Word but not doing it (James 1:22; 4:17).
▶ Saying, "I have not sinned" (1 John 1:8).
▶ Thinking I am something I am really not (Gal. 6:3).
▶ Thinking I am wise in the things of the world (1 Cor. 3:18–19).
▶ Thinking I will not reap what I sow (Gal. 6:7).
▶ Thinking that ungodly people who live lives of sin will share in God's kingdom (1 Cor. 6:9–10).
▶ Thinking I can hang out with bad people and they won't have bad influence on me (1 Cor. 15:33).
▶ Thinking I can be a good Christian and still hurt others by what I say (James 1:26).[3]

Quitting sin involves accepting forgiveness and breaking free of the bondage of past sin and guilt. Freedom comes through Christ—not through ritual, religion, or effort. Walking in freedom from sin requires that both spouses pray, read the Word, and worship together. Each makes a commitment or covenant sealed in the power of God's Spirit to walk righteously with one another. Make the following covenant to one another:

> I covenant in love and in Jesus' name to admit and quit my sin. I claim the power to walk in the freedom of His truth and to break every past bondage of sin. I ask and receive the forgiveness of Jesus Christ for my sins through His shed blood. I covenant to pray, read the Word, and worship faithfully with you. I ask your forgiveness, and I forgive you of any past hurt. I will never again mention this sin or any past sin you have committed against me. May Christ seal this covenant of love in my heart.

The only way to keep the wall of unconfessed sin from being rebuilt is to forgive and forget the past sin. Most couples can accept the forgiveness part but protest that forgetting past hurt and sin against them is impossible. In forgiveness, God eradicates the memory of sin, "For I will forgive their wickedness and will remember their sins no more" (Jer. 31:34; Heb. 8:12). How do couples demonstrate that they have forgiven and forgotten? They refuse to bring up past sin. They do not use past sin as a weapon of accusation or as a means of condemnation against their spouses. They avoid mentioning a past

134

sin when they are angry. They do not expose a spouse's past sin to anyone else.

Repenting of the Wall of Unconfessed Sin

I repent of all my sin, Lord Jesus. For the sins of commission and omission I repent. I have sinned against You, God, and I repent of my sin. For any transgression of Your law, I repent. For hurting others, including my mate, I repent. For every sin I remember and all those I do not remember, I repent.

For every sin of my mouth, my mind, my emotions, and my body, I repent. Knowing that my heart is deceitfully wicked, I ask Your mercy and the cleansing of Your blood. Though my sins are as scarlet they will be white as snow in You, Lord Jesus.

I repent of my sins before my mate. I am a sinner saved by grace through faith in Jesus Christ. I need Your grace because I cannot forgive or save myself. With You, Jesus, I am a lost sheep who has gone astray. Forgive, save, redeem, and restore me, Jesus, my Savior.

—Amen

Shout these praises with your spouse:

Praise the LORD, I tell myself;
with my whole heart, I will praise his holy name.

Praise the Lord, I tell myself,
  and never forget the good things he does
    for me.
He forgives all my sins
  and heals all my diseases.
He ransoms me from death
  and surrounds me with love and tender
    mercies.
He fills my life with good things.
  My youth is renewed like the eagle's!
                    —PSALM 103:1–5, NLT

THE WALL OF
UNDIGNIFIED COMMUNICATION

YOU MAY BE praying for conviction. Conviction will not be pleasant or neat. When the Holy Spirit convicts one of sin the process may involve turmoil, resistance, and very messy and unpleasant communication. At times, those who are under conviction project their guilt on others. You may become the target of blame and condemnation. Such resistance to the Spirit's conviction will build another wall—the wall of undignified communication.

This brings us to a discussion of the tongue. An abusive, unkind tongue can quickly build a spiritual wall between spouses that results in ugly put downs, profanity, verbal abuse, and bitter words. Does your communication with your husband contain any of the following elements?

Profanity   Angry expressions
Verbal abuse   Demeaning remarks

Put downs	Unkind words
Disrespectful tone	Hurtful language
Accusations	Cajoling or nagging
Condemnation	Stony silence

I know one wife who refuses to accept any blame, put downs, or verbal abuse from her husband by tugging on her ear lobe any time he starts with any of the above types of negative communication. What does this non-verbal action mean? By her actions, she is saying, "This is an ear. But you are misusing it as a garbage can. This ear is not a garbage can, and I refuse to allow garbage to enter it."

After angry, profane, and vicious verbal exchanges, some couples try to reconcile by saying, "I really didn't mean what I said." But if one didn't mean it, why was it said? Jesus observed, "Listen and understand, What goes into a man's mouth does not make him 'unclean,' but what comes out of his mouth, that is what makes him 'unclean'" (Matt. 15:10). "The good man brings good things out of the good stored up in his heart, and the evil man brings evil things out of the evil stored up in his heart. For out of the overflow of his heart his mouth speaks" (Luke 6:45).

One wife, filled with boldness in the Spirit when her husband released a stream of profanity directed at her, had the courage to say, "I rebuke you in the name of Jesus Christ. Shut your mouth." Startled, he stormed out of the room and has not cursed her again to this day.

Are the tongues in your marriage gracious or poisonous? How can sweet prayers come out of a mouth one moment and libelous slander the next?

James asks, "With the tongue we praise our Lord and Father, and with it we curse men, who have been made in God's likeness. Out of the same mouth come praise and cursing. My brothers, this should not be. Can both fresh water and salt water flow from the same spring?" (James 3:9–11).

There is no point in praying together if the same tongues begin to curse one another after the amen! If the wall of undignified communication is to be torn down for prayer and praise to be released in marriage, then both spouses must control their tongues. If you control yours and your husband does not, continue to pray for him in this way:

Lord Jesus, I bind my husband's tongue to Your will. I release in him and me all anger, bitterness, and poisonous words. I bind his thoughts and words to whatever is pure, lovely, admirable, excellent and praise-worthy.

—Amen

Pray this over your husband as he sleeps and aloud when he begins to speak angrily. Remember, God does not require you to listen to your husband's abusive language. If he will not control his tongue, leave the room. And if he continues to abuse you verbally, get support and help immediately. You may have to separate physically until his tongue comes under control through the Holy Spirit.

If you cannot control your tongue, pray the same prayer for yourself. Remember, in the power of the tongue is life and death (Prov. 18:21). Choose to speak life and not death into your marriage and your spiritual life. Repent to one another and ask forgiveness for hurtful things you have said in the past to one another. Covenant to use your tongues for blessing one another in the future.

> ▶ *Repenting of the Wall of Undignified Communication* ◀

Lord, I ask You to guard my tongue and my mate's tongue in this marriage. I declare that in our tongues are both life and death. Holy Spirit, put the words in my mouth so that only living waters flow from me, refreshing my mate.

Jesus, silence his/her tongue when any word of death is formed there. May every negative word we utter in marriage be immediately rebuked and repented of in Jesus' name.

Lord Jesus, I know that we will be judged by every word we speak. So silence our fiery tongues and give us Your words of honey. Give us soft answers to turn away each other's anger. Help us to form positive, affirming, and loving words with our lips. Grant us the wisdom to know when to be silent. In Jesus' name, we pull down the wall of undignified communication and replace our word with Your Word. May the words of our mouths and the meditations of our hearts be acceptable in Your sight.

—Amen

Ж

Pray this verse with your mate:

> May the words of my mouth and the medita-
> tion of my heart be pleasing in your sight, O
> Lord, my Rock and my Redeemer.
> —PSALM 19:14

THE WALL OF UNFEELING RESPONSES

YEARS AGO I heard Joyce Landorf give a talk that impressed me with this truth: There are some irregular people in our lives. Who is an irregular person? An irregular person is one with whom we must relate—like a spouse, child, or parent—who has no sensitivity to our feelings. Such a person's responses simply do not fit with what we say or feel.

For example, you may say, "I was really hurt by what you said." To which your irregular person might respond, "What's for dinner?" Crying, you may say, "The cat was killed when it was hit by a car." And your irregular person responds, "Hope the mess isn't still on the road."

Irregular spouses do not communicate on the same wavelength. As a result, the sensitive, feeling partner often experiences hurt as a result of the unfeeling responses of her partner. She may put up a wall and conclude, "He doesn't care about my feelings." He may care but be unable or unwilling to work at becoming sensitive.

There are ways to avoid this wall or to tear it down if it begins to arise. Here are some simple steps:

140

1. *Identify and communicate your feelings.* Let your husband know how you feel and what you desire to communicate about your feelings when you pray together. For example, "I feel hurt when you ignore my desire to pray."

2. *Use sentence prayers that communicate feelings.* Together, complete and pray these sentences aloud:

   > Lord, I feel angry when...
   > Lord, I feel hurt when...
   > Lord, I feel pain when...
   > Lord, I rejoice when...
   > Lord, I am hopeful when...
   > Lord, I feel loved when...

   Remember to express your feelings in prayer in a way that does not project blame on God or on your spouse. For example, "Lord, I feel angry when my husband should be giving me attention" is a prayer that projects blame. The same feeling can be expressed in a prayer like this: "Lord, I feel angry when I need attention from my husband but my expectation is not met."

3. *Don't bury or repress your feelings.* Some wives decide to bury their feelings, thinking that they should not have certain feelings or that they should feel differently than they do. Share your feelings with God in prayer and let your husband hear your prayer.

4. *Ask your husband to repeat back to you what you just said.* Irregular people who respond with unfeeling responses often never really hear what's being said by their spouses. They may be thinking about their own needs. Or their minds may be miles away. Whatever the reason, the irregular person often never listens closely to what is being said. When you need your spouse to hear your feelings so that you can genuinely pray what you feel, ask him for responses to these questions:

> What did you hear me say?
> What do you understand my feelings to be?
> Are you willing to pray with me about my feelings?

> If your husband does not accurately describe your statements or feelings, then restate them until he understands you clearly.

Steve continually shared in our men's group about his wife's intensity in prayer. "She overflows with all kinds of feelings. She may laugh and cry all in the same prayer time together. I can't handle all of her feelings when we pray," Steve would confide.

"How do you feel when she prays with such intensity of emotions?" I asked.

"Inadequate and unable to pray like her. I just don't see why she has to be so intense. I like to pray short prayers that go straight to the point, but she goes on for what seems like hour after hour, never really saying anything," Steve complained.

"So, what do you want to do?" I probed.

"Her praying wears me out. I would rather pray with a group of men than with my wife, and that makes me feel badly," he confided.

"What happens when you share how you feel with her?" I asked.

"She gets upset, saying that I don't want to pray with her. I do, but I feel so emotionally drained. Usually I avoid praying with my wife unless we do so right before we leave the house. That way I know she has to stop praying soon since we have someplace to go."

Be careful about overwhelming your husband with feelings when you pray. He may not feel with the same intensity as you do, but refuse to allow that to be a barrier to praying together. Ask him if he feels uncomfortable when you share your feelings in prayer.

Seek to understand one another's comfort level when you pray; allow one another to grow together in prayer instead of pushing each other to sharing that which may be uncomfortable.

One wife confided that she felt it was her duty to get her husband out of his comfort zone when they prayed together. She wanted to push him into depths of prayer he had never experienced. However, he put up a wall of unfeeling responses and began to withdraw. Thinking he was backsliding, she called me to ask what she should do.

My response was simple, "Back off. Stop pushing him to pray about things and to express feelings he does not feel comfortable with. Let him grow at a pace that God sets—not that which you want to set."

A few months later she told me after a church service, "My husband is really taking a lead in our prayer life since I backed off. Thanks for the insight. He is now growing spiritually in areas I never dreamed possible."

▶ *Repenting of the Wall of Unfeeling Responses* ◀

Jesus, when my mate responds to me with a lack of sensitivity, caring, and love, empower me to respond with a love deeper than he/she can comprehend. Take my focus away from my feelings. Tune my heart to Yours that I may feel what You feel, be brokenhearted by what breaks Your heart, and love all that You love.

I know, Lord Jesus, that only You know how I really feel. So, Holy Spirit, speak to my heart, removing all insecurity, inferiority, and unwillingness to risk. Make of me a wounded healer so that when others are unfeeling, I may feel and heal with Your compassion and comfort.

Jesus, in Your name I pull down the wall of unfeeling responses, and I take upon me Your mantle of vulnerability and trust. I will risk being hurt in my marriage so that I can remain close to my mate and to You.

—Amen

M

Pray this scripture with your spouse:

My eyes are always looking to the Lord for
> help,
> for he alone can rescue me from the traps
> of my enemies.

Turn to me and have mercy on me,
> for I am alone and in deep distress.
My problems go from bad to worse.
> Oh, save me from them all!
Feel my pain and see my trouble.
> Forgive all my sins.
See how many enemies I have,
> and how viciously they hate me!
Protect me! Rescue my life from them!
> Do not let me be disgraced, for I trust in
> you.
May integrity and honesty protect me,
> for I put my hope in you.
>   —Psalm 25:15–21, nlt

From a Husband's Perspective

When spiritual walls of unconfessed sin, undignified communication, and unfeeling responses go up in a marriage, some of the viewpoints I have heard husbands express to me over the years are as follows:

> ▶ I feel guilty every time I pray with my wife. It's easier to avoid praying with her than to experience guilt all the time.
> ▶ I just want her forgiveness for my sin. I want to know I am forgiven and we can go on.
> ▶ When I'm not right with God, it's very hard to

pray with my wife. I need to get right before I can pray with her.

➤ She wants me to bare all in prayer. I have some areas of my life that I must deal with in my relationship with God—not her.

➤ I wish I could confess sin when I pray with my wife without her being judgmental or hurt after we pray.

➤ My wife prays too long.

➤ I am so emotionally drained after we pray that I feel terrible. Aren't you supposed to feel better, not worse, after you pray with your wife?

➤ My wife says things when she is angry that really hurt me. After her verbal barrage I don't want to pray with her.

➤ I know my foul language has hurt my wife. And I don't know how to pray with holy language. So it's easier not to pray than to feel like a hypocrite when I pray.

➤ I don't know how to respond to my wife's feelings when she prays. And when I don't respond the way she expects, she really gets upset with me.

➤ My wife says things, and I have no idea where she's coming from. By the time I figure it out, I'm in big trouble with her.

➤ It's easier to endure her frustration with me for not praying with her than to handle her hurt from what I say honestly and frankly in prayer.

When sin barriers go up in a couple's spiritual life, they cannot be ignored. Time does not heal, and hurt doesn't just go away. Confession, repentance, and forgiveness are necessary.

So, what does the Bridegroom ask us to do when

we are tempted to build these walls?

THE BRIDEGROOM'S PERSPECTIVE

JESUS INSISTS THAT we deal thoroughly with sin. In fact, the first words He spoke at the beginning of His ministry were, "Repent, for the kingdom of heaven is near" (Matt. 4:17). Jesus links being forgiven by God with our willingness to forgive others. "For if you forgive men when they sin against you, your heavenly Father will also forgive you. But if you do not forgive men their sins, your Father will not forgive your sins" (Matt. 6:14–15).

The walls of unconfessed sin are torn down and shattered by repentance and forgiveness. We have no right to hold onto our sins or to hold onto the sins of others against us. As your Bridegroom, Jesus says to you, "This is my body given for you; do this in remembrance of me...This cup is the new covenant in my blood, which is poured out for you" (Luke 22:19–20). "This is my blood of the covenant, which is poured out for many for the forgiveness of sins" (Matt. 26:28). He longs to forgive you if you will repent, tearing down the walls of unconfessed sin, undignified communication, and unfeeling responses.

The Bridegroom also warns us about our words. Guard your tongue as well as your heart. Listen to His words, "For out of the overflow of the heart the mouth speaks...For by your words you will be acquitted, and by your words you will be condemned" (Matt. 12:34, 37).

Release whatever sin or offense you may be harboring. Control your mouth so that only what is edifying comes out. Be sensitive to the feelings of your husband even when his sins are overt and ugly.

Remember the woman taken in adultery? Though she had sinned and broken the Law, she was treated with mercy by Jesus. Accord your husband the same measure of mercy that Jesus gives you. Jesus instructs, "Blessed are the merciful, for they will be shown mercy" (Matt. 5:7).

KEYS TO KEEPING THE WALLS DOWN AND HAVING EFFECTIVE PRAYER TOGETHER

WE HAVE EXPLORED how to recognize and tear down these walls, but how do we move beyond building these walls in the first place? From time to time we will sin, say something hurtful, or respond with insensitivity. You or your husband could be tempted to put up any one of these walls at any time. But there are keys to avoid putting up walls that hinder your prayers and spiritual sharing together.

Key #1 — Quickly Repent

When you sin against God, repent quickly. When you find yourself sinning against your husband, repent before that sin can take root in your life. For example, Paul writes, "In your anger do not sin. Do not let the sun go down while you are still angry" (Eph. 4:26). Unconfessed sin acts like a magnet attracting other sinful behaviors to it. Lack of repentance dulls and even sears our conscience so that sinning is easier the next time. Unconfessed sin also grows mistrust and lack of communication in a marriage. It stifles effective prayer and starts us on a course of prayerlessness.

148

Key #2 — Listen Before Speaking or Acting

Use prayer as a time to listen to God and to your spouse. Time your prayers. What percentage of time do you spend listening to God compared to the time you spend talking to Him?

Obviously, if you spend most of your time talking, you will hear very little. If God's Spirit is trying to convict you of sin, you need to hear His voice. Hebrews warns, "Today, if you hear his voice, do not harden your hearts as you did in rebellion" (Heb. 3:15).

Listening to God's voice in prayer and in the Word will protect you from sin. "I have hidden your word in my heart that I might not sin against you" (Ps. 119:11).

Listening will also help you to control destructive anger. James writes, "Everyone should be quick to listen, slow to speak, and slow to become angry" (James 1:19).

Try this: You and your husband read aloud Psalm 1 in unison. Close your eyes and sit silently, listening to God speak to you through His Word. Share with each other the phrase that spoke most directly to your own heart and why.

Pray that the blessing of Psalm 1 will be in each other's life. Then silently listen to God's Spirit speak to you about how to implement Psalm 1 in your lives. After five to ten minutes share with each other what God has spoken to you.

Key #3 — Daily Confess Sin to One Another

Incorporate confession and repentance into your

prayer life together as a couple. Repenting daily leaves no opportunity for sin to crouch at the door of your life (Gen. 4:7).

Daily confession leads to ongoing fellowship between spouses that cannot be broken. "But if we walk in the light, as he is in the light, we have fellowship with one another, and the blood of Jesus, his Son, purifies us from every sin. If we claim to be without sin, we deceive ourselves and the truth is not in us. If we confess our sins, he is faithful and just and will forgive us our sins and purify us from all unrighteousness" (1 John 1:7–9).

Finally, confession brings healing into our lives and our relationships.

James writes, "Therefore confess your sins to each other and pray for each other so that you may be healed" (James 5:16).

Do you want a restored prayer life with your husband? Confess your sins to one another daily. Do you want to pray effectively in faith with power? Confess your sins to each other daily. Do you want to enjoy a healed and restored relationship? Confess your sins to each other daily.

Key #4 — Guard Your Tongue

Use your tongue for prayer and praise. Avoid putting your spouse down. Let your tongue be used to edify one another (Prov. 18:21). In prayer, thank God for your spouse.

Key #5 — Refuse to Dump on One Another

Remember that your partner may not be able to

handle all your feelings, hurts, and needs at one time. Only God can care for everything that you need: "Casting all your care upon him; for he careth for you" (1 Pet. 5:7, KJV).

Key #6 — Pray for Sensitivity and Kindness

In a marriage counselors' training seminar years ago, Wayne Oates was asked, "What is the most important advise you give to couples in counseling?"

I was expecting some profound spiritual answer like, "Pray for one another," or "Love God and each other," or "Always forgive each other." Oates simply said, "Be kind to one another." (See Ephesians 4:32.)

Why do we tend to hurt most those we love most? Why do we treat strangers at times with more civility and kindness than our own mates? Pray for God to fill you with His Spirit of comfort, who is always kind and sensitive to our needs and concerns.

In summary, we have learned the following:

> ▶ Tearing down the wall of unconfessed sin involves admitting our sin, quitting it, and then forgetting it.
> ▶ Avoiding self-deception keeps us from building the wall of unconfessed sin.
> ▶ We must forgive and forget past sin in order to keep the spiritual walls down between spouses.
> ▶ We do not have to listen to the garbage of undignified communication from a mate.
> ▶ Guarding our tongues and speaking what is positive, not negative, keeps the walls down in marriage.
> ▶ If a spouse is one's irregular person, we can

overcome walls by expressing our feelings clearly and directly.

➤ We pray most effectively with our spouses when we quickly repent, daily confess sin to one another, guard our tongues, refuse to dump on one another, and pray for sensitivity and kindness.

Almighty God, I surrender my tongue to You. Use my mouth to build up—not tear down. Teach us in marriage how to respect and honor each other with our words and actions. I confess my sins. Cleanse me with Your blood. Make me sensitive, Father, to You and not to my own selfish feelings.
—Amen

Now we can turn to a final section of prayers that you can pray for your husband and with your husband that span the depths of confession, blessing, intercession, agreement, fasting, and praying while absent from one another.

Lord Jesus, think on me and purge away my sin;
  From earth-born passions set me free and make me
pure within.
  Lord Jesus, think on me, with care and woe oppressed;
  Let me Thy loving servant be and gain Thy promised
rest.
  Lord Jesus, think on me nor let me go astray;
  Through darkness and perplexity point Thou the heav-
enly way.
  Lord Jesus, think on me, that when the flood is past, I
may the eternal brightness see and share Thy joy at last.

—SYNESIUS OF CYRENE
4TH CENTURY A.D.

7

CONFESSION: REPENTANCE
THAT HEALS MARRIAGES

JAMES WEPT AS he told Rebecca of his prayerlessness. No, he hadn't prayed for months. The only prayers he had prayed were blessings before the meals. He had not prayed with her or for her. In fact, when everyone was praying at church, he was thinking about the upcoming Sunday afternoon football games. When she prayed before they fell asleep at night, he went over the next day's to-do list in his mind.

So what brought about this wall-shattering confession on his part? Rebecca had attended a prayer seminar at church that taught her how to pray Scripture. One passage that had particularly impacted her prayer life was Psalm 51—David's prayer of repentance after his adultery with Bathsheba. One evening she prayed this psalm aloud as James listened. As she prayed her confession, her tender and broken spirit had touched

James' heart. He began to weep. He started confessing his prayerlessness to her, which of course she was aware of but never condemned. Her contrite spirit had torn down the spiritual walls between them.

John writes, "If we confess our sins, he is faithful and just and will forgive us our sins and purify us from all unrighteousness" (1 John 1:9). Your confession does not depend on your husband. Whether he is contrite or not does not affect your confession. Any sins against him, others, or God need to be cleansed from your life regardless of your husband's repentance or lack of it. At times, wives may feel that they are justified in being unrepentant because their husbands are so arrogant and rebellious against God. Our only right is to repent. God will deal with your husband if he refuses to confess his sins.

Do not react to your husband's attitudes and thus cause a wall to go up between you and God. You are not the Holy Spirit. God does not need you to convict your husband of his sin or to confess his sins for him. Humble yourself and confess your own sins.

Long before James ever repented, Rebecca was confessing her sins. Nothing pulls down spiritual walls between you and your husband like prayers of repentance.

Before praying repentance, memorize the scriptures given in this chapter. Get the Word in you so that you can pray the Word out of you.

Repentance and confession speak of turning away from sin and agreeing with God. The Greek word for *repentance* (*metanoia*) means "to turn away from iniquity and sin," while the Greek word for *confess* (*homologeo*) means "to agree with." In other words, we agree with the way God sees us. So we not only confess or agree with His conviction of our sin but also His affirmation of our sonship in Christ.

Confession not only agrees with God about your sin, but also agrees with His promises to forgive and cleanse you of sin. Repentance not only turns you away from sin but also turns you toward righteousness. Consider this:

In repentance we turn from:	We turn to:
Sin	Surrender
Self	Christ
Rebellion	Submission
Alienation	Relationship
Enmity	Reconciliation
Brokenness	Reconciliation
Affliction	Healing
Hate	Love
Division	Unity
Turmoil	Peace

Look over the above list, and circle the areas that still need repentance in your life. Underline the areas for which you truly repent and for which you praise God for His forgiveness.

THE WORD ABOUT REPENTANCE AND CONFESSION

IN HIS BOOK, *Prayer: Key to Revival,* David (Paul) Yonggi Cho stated:

When you come in contact with God in your time of prayer, the first thing you feel in your heart as you enter into His divine presence is the realization of your sin. No one can sense pride in the presence of a holy God. Once you sense your lack of natural qualifications to be in His Holy Presence, you will begin to confess your sin and humble yourself before God.[1]

The Bible is filled with many passages that speak about our need to repent and confess our sins— both to *God* and to *each other*. As a couple, read together the following verses. Share the passages that speak most to your hearts, and explain why:

If my people, who are called by my name, will humble themselves and pray and seek my face and turn from their wicked ways, then will I hear from heaven and will forgive their sin and will heal their land.
—2 CHRONICLES 7:14

For I take no pleasure in the death of anyone, declares the Sovereign LORD. Repent and live!
—EZEKIEL 18:32

I confess my iniquity; I am troubled by my sin.
—PSALM 38:18

From that time on Jesus began to preach, "Repent, for the kingdom of heaven is near."
—MATTHEW 4:17

Also I say unto you, Whosoever shall confess me before men, him shall the Son of man also confess before the angels of God.

—LUKE 12:8, KJV

I tell you, no! But unless you repent, you too will all perish.

—LUKE 13:3

Peter replied, "Repent and be baptized, every one of you, in the name of Jesus Christ so that your sins may be forgiven. And you will receive the gift of the Holy Spirit."

—ACTS 2:38

Repent, then, and turn to God, so that your sins may be wiped out, that times of refreshing may come from the Lord.

—ACTS 3:19

For it is with your heart that you believe and are justified, and it is with your mouth that you confess and are saved.

—ROMANS 10:10

Godly sorrow brings repentance that leads to salvation and leaves no regret, but worldly sorrow brings death.

—2 CORINTHIANS 7:10

Nevertheless, God's solid foundation stands firm, sealed with this inscription: "The Lord knows those who are his," and, "Everyone who confesses the name of the Lord must turn away from wickedness."

—2 TIMOTHY 2:19

Come near to God and he will come near to you. Wash your hands, you sinners, and purify your hearts, you double-minded.

—JAMES 4:8

Grieve, mourn and wail. Change your laughter to mourning and your joy to gloom.

—JAMES 4:9

Humble yourselves before the Lord, and he will lift you up.

—JAMES 4:10

Therefore confess your sins to each other and pray for each other so that you may be healed. The prayer of a righteous man is powerful and effective.

—JAMES 5:16

If we confess our sins, he is faithful and just and will forgive us our sins and purify us from all unrighteousness.

—1 JOHN 1:9

Those whom I love I rebuke and discipline. So be earnest, and repent.

—REVELATION 3:19

PRAYERS OF CONFESSION

THE FOLLOWING PRAYERS can be prayed either for or with your husband.

Pray them aloud in his hearing. If he is willing to do so, pray them aloud together.

Confessing My Sin

Pray Psalm 51 aloud in the hearing of your husband as your personal prayer of confession. *Put your name in place of the personal pronouns.* This psalm was written by David soon after the prophet Nathan confronted him regarding his adultery with Bathsheba.

Have mercy on me, O God,
  because of your unfailing love.
Because of your great compassion,
  blot out the stain of my sins.
Wash me clean from my guilt.
  Purify me from my sin.

For I recognize my shameful deeds—
  they haunt me day and night.
Against you, and you alone, have I sinned;
  I have done what is evil in your sight.
You will be proved right in what you say,
  and your judgment against me is just.

For I was born a sinner—
  yes, from the moment my mother
    conceived me.
But you desire honesty from the heart,
  so you can teach me to be wise in my
    inmost being.

Purify me from my sins, and I will be clean;
  wash me, and I will be whiter than snow.
Oh, give me back my joy again;
  you have broken me—
    now let me rejoice.

Don't keep looking at my sins.
  Remove the stain of my guilt.
Create in me a clean heart, O God.
  Renew a right spirit within me.
Do not banish me from your presence,
  and don't take your Holy Spirit from me.
Restore to me again the joy of your
    salvation,
  and make me willing to obey you.
Then I will teach your ways to sinners,
  and they will return to you.
Forgive me for shedding blood, O God who
    saves;
  then I will joyfully sing of your
    forgiveness. Amen.
                    —PSALM 51:1–14, NLT

Confessing Our Sin

Pray Ezra 9:6–9, 13, 15, in unison with your husband.
*Put both of your names in place of the personal
pronouns.*

O my God, I am utterly ashamed; I blush to lift
up my face to you. For our sins are piled higher
than our heads, and our guilt has reached to
the heavens. Our whole history has been one
of great sin. That is why we and our [leaders
and our pastors] have been at the mercy of the
[world]. We have been killed, captured, robbed,
and disgraced, just as we are today.

But now we have been given a brief
moment of grace, for the LORD our God has
allowed a few of us to survive as a remnant.

He has given us security in this holy place. Our God has brightened our eyes and granted us some relief from our slavery.

For we were slaves [of sin], but in his unfailing love our God did not abandon us in our slavery... Now we are being punished because of our wickedness and our great guilt. But we have actually been punished far less than we deserve, for you, our God, have allowed some of us to survive as a remnant...

O Lord, God of Israel, you are just. We stand before you in our guilt as nothing but an escaped remnant, though in such a condition none of us can stand in your presence. Amen.

—Ezra 9:6–9, 13, 15, nlt

Seeking God's Mercy

Pray Daniel 9:16–19 in unison with your husband. *Put both of your names in place of the personal pronouns.*

In view of all your faithful mercies, Lord, please turn your furious anger away from [our home], your holy mountain [in our neighborhood]. All the [neighbors] mock [us], your people, because of our sins and the sins of our ancestors. O our God, hear your servant's prayer! Listen as I plead. For your own sake, Lord, smile again on your desolate sanctuary. O my God, listen to me and hear my request. Open your eyes and see our wretchedness. See how [our lives] lie in ruins—for everyone knows that [we are] yours. We do not ask

because we deserve help, but because you are
so merciful. O Lord, hear. O Lord, forgive. O
Lord, listen and act! For your own sake, O my
God, do not delay, for your people and [our
home] bear your name. Amen.

—DANIEL 9:16–19, NLT

Confessing His Knowledge of My Inmost Being

Pray Psalm 139 in unison with your husband. *You
may want to replace the personal pronouns with the
name of your husband or with the names of your
children.*

O LORD, you have examined my heart
  and know everything about me.
You know when I sit down or stand up.
  You know my every thought when far
    away.
You chart the path ahead of me
  and tell me where to stop and rest.
  Every moment you know where I am.
You know what I am going to say
  even before I say it, LORD.
You both precede and follow me.
  You place your hand of blessing on my
    head.
Such knowledge is too wonderful for me,
  too great for me to know!

I can never escape from your spirit!
  I can never get away from your
    presence!
If I go up to heaven, you are there;

If I go down to the place of the dead, you
    are there.
If I ride the wings of the morning,
    if I dwell by the farthest oceans,
even there your hand will guide me,
    and your strength will support me.
I could ask the darkness to hide me
    and the light around me to become
        night—
    but even in darkness I cannot hide from
        you.
To you the night shines as bright as day.
    Darkness and light are both alike to you.

You made all the delicate, inner parts of my
    body
    and knit me together in my mother's
        womb.
Thank you for making me so wonderfully
    complex!
    Your workmanship is marvelous—and
        how well I know it.
You watched me as I was being formed in
    utter seclusion,
    as I was woven together in the dark of the
        womb.
You saw me before I was born.
    Every day of my life was recorded in your
        book.
Every moment was laid out
    before a single day had passed.

How precious are your thoughts about me,
    O God!

They are innumerable!
I can't even count them;
   they outnumber the grains of sand!
And when I wake up in the morning,
   you are still with me . . .

Search me, O God, and know my heart;
   test me and know my thoughts.
Point out anything in me that offends you,
   and lead me along the path of everlasting
     life. Amen.
                —PSALM 139:1–18, 23–24, NLT

REPENTANCE: TEARING DOWN THE WALLS

A HUSBAND AND a wife are two people who have become one in Christ. Jesus says, "For this reason a man will leave his father and mother and be united to his wife, and the two will become one flesh. So they are no longer two, but one. Therefore what God has joined together let man not separate" (Mark 10:7–9). The walls we build that spiritually divide us must be destroyed. Christ intends for marriage to be a spiritual union that models His relationship with the church (Eph. 5). So who brings down the walls? How are they shattered and destroyed?

Our answer is found in Ephesians 2:14: "For he [Christ] is our peace, who has made the two one and has destroyed the barrier, the dividing wall of hostility."

Now, although you may pull down a wall, your husband may still have a spiritual barrier erected between himself and you. Or he may pull down a wall while you are still maintaining a spiritual barrier. It is necessary for both of you, as one in Christ, to come to Him in repentant prayer, and He will destroy the walls.

Neither one of you can do it alone, but praying together in Christ will shatter any and all walls between you. You may protest, saying, "We don't feel like praying this way," or "We don't feel like we are one in Christ." Feelings are not always an accurate measure of truth. In marriage, the spiritual reality is oneness in Christ. So you can pray together in spite of your feelings. What? Do something that contradicts your feelings? Absolutely. Your prayer life and spiritual life together are more important than how you feel at the moment. Feelings can and do change. Absolute truth never changes—it's true for all times, all people, and in all situations.

God declares that in marriage you and your husband are one. That truth doesn't change one morning if you wake up feeling unloving that day. That truth has not been changed if you haven't prayed together for a week, month, or even years. Spiritual walls that have been in place for ages can be shattered in a twinkling of an eye by Christ—He is your peace, the destroyer of the dividing wall of hostility.

PRAYING WITH POWER AND WONDERFUL RESULTS

WITH REPENTANCE AND confession the spiritual walls in marriage come tumbling down like the walls of Jericho. Healing is released for the marriage relationship and for spiritual growth together. As a couple prays, they will encounter the power of God's Spirit working in and through them. Before prayer changes *things, people* will be changed (2 Cor. 3:18).

For years, Judi and I had prayed together only sporadically and without power or effectiveness. Then a crisis arose. Our daughter began to associate with a group of friends whose life directions were opposed to the gospel. They used drugs, listened to offensive forms of rock music, hung out in clubs, and became involved in many forms of rebellion against all authority figures—parents, teachers, police, and others.

The crisis we faced of losing not only a relationship with our daughter but also the possibility of her turning away from God caused us to crash-dive to our knees. In our pride, we had thought that having a rebellious teenager could never happen to us. We believed ourselves to have been good parents who raised Amy with the right values and morality.

But she was making choices that would lead to destruction in her life unless we intervened. All of our efforts to discipline and correct her failed miserably. The advice of counselors and friends was not working. We were desperate. That crisis shattered our spiritual walls and brought us together in agreement for our daughter's salvation, deliverance, and protection. At times God may use a crisis to drive a couple to their knees. He didn't cause the crisis, but we learned the truth that "in all things God works for the good of those who love him, who have been called according to his purpose" (Rom. 8:28).

Praying together we saw God do powerful things with wonderful results. Time and time again, through prayer the Holy Spirit led us to the dangerous places where our daughter had put herself so that we could bring her out of clubs, parties, and harmful relationships. God gave us just the right words to say to her that encouraged her and showed her our love. When we might have disciplined her harshly or said hurtful things to her, God controlled our tongues through prayer.

One night after Judi and I prayed, I fell into a restless sleep tossing and turning while Judi continued to pray. Suddenly, she shook me awake and said, "Go quickly now to Don's house. Amy is in trouble. Bring her home." I dressed quickly, drove to Don's house, and discovered that Amy was struggling with some decisions that would have been very destructive to her. Thankfully, she came home with me, though she was angry and upset with me for spoiling her night.

Over a period of months, the Holy Spirit began to change us and Amy so that she was restored to our family, the family of God, and to God's plan and purpose for her life. Today she and her husband have a wonderful ministry and a beautiful son. They love and serve God. A couple praying together will see God do powerful and wonderful things.

We have seen our sons dedicate their lives to the Lord and serve Him with their respective careers because God was faithful to answer the prayers we prayed. Our prayers were random and lacked polish, discipline, and maturity. In spite of our weak efforts, God was faithful, and He answered our prayers no matter how undisciplined we were. Today we regret not giving God more opportunity to change us and our family through prayer. We have found ourselves repenting through the years for all that did not happen because we did not pray!

Stop missing what God desires to do in and through you as a couple. After tearing down the spiritual walls between you, pray continually. "And pray in the Spirit on all occasions with all kinds of prayers and requests. With this in mind, be alert and always keep on praying for all the saints" (Eph. 6:18).

> Therefore, since we are surrounded by such a great cloud of witnesses, let us throw off everything that hinders and the sin that so easily entangles, and let us run with persever- ance the race marked out for us. Let us fix our eyes on Jesus, the author and perfector of our faith, who for the joy set before him endured the cross, scorning its shame, and sat down at the right hand of the throne of God.
> —HEBREWS 12:1–2

FIFTY WAYS TO KEEP SPIRITUAL WALLS PULLED DOWN AS A COUPLE

> In the same way, the Spirit helps us in our weakness. We do not know what we ought to pray, but the Spirit himself intercedes for us with groans that words cannot express. And he who searches our hearts knows the mind of the Spirit, because the Spirit intercedes for the saints in accordance with God's will.
> —ROMANS 8:26–27

Let me suggest many different ways you and your husband can pray together. No style or way is sacred. Remember to listen more to God's voice than to each other's. Don't be *self*-conscious—Be *God*-conscious. Let the Spirit pray through you when you do not know how to pray.

1. Pray, read, meditate upon, and memorize Scripture together.
2. Have daily devotions together.
3. Write down your prayers for and with each other.
4. Keep a spiritual journal together.
5. Pray silently together.
6. Pray aloud together.
7. Pray together in the car while driving to your destination.
8. Sing your prayers together.
9. Daily recite your blessings and God's answers to your prayers.
10. Use a concordance to search the Scriptures for...

   ▶ All the promises of God
   ▶ All the prayers in the Bible
   ▶ All the verses about prayer in the Bible
   ▶ All the times God answered prayer in the Bible

11. Together read a Christian book, taking turns reading to each other.
12. Pray together in a worship service.
13. Pray together while taking a walk.
14. Pray together after making love.
15. Keep a prayer list for the needs of others and pray over it regularly.
16. Keep a list of each other's prayer needs; freely add to one another's list. Remember to give praise when prayers are answered.
17. Join a prayer group or go to a prayer service together.

18. Write prayers for one another and share them.
19. Find a book of prayers in your Christian bookstore and pray through it together.
20. Attend a prayer retreat together.
21. Pray and fast together one day, one week, or even longer.
22. Confess your sins to one another daily.
23. Make a praise list and pray through it.
24. Lay hands on one another and pray for each other.
25. Pray in the Spirit for one another.
26. Do a spiritual map of your community or region and pray down the strongholds together.
27. Anoint one another with oil and pray for healing.
28. Pack prayer requests in one another's clothing when you travel.
29. Call one another during the day and pray for each other over the phone.
30. Ask a spiritually mature couple to share the ways they pray together and grow spiritually closer.
31. Ask your pastor to pray a blessing over you.
32. Go to the elders together for anointing with oil and prayer.
33. Spend time together praying at the altar of your church.
34. Visit your neighbors and ask how you might pray for them.

35. Pray for Christian leaders together—teachers, missionaries, pastors, youth workers, preachers, and prophets.

36. Pray over one another's ears, mouths, and eyes to protect what is taken into each other's lives.

37. Turn off the television or radio and pray.

38. Replace your favorite weekly television program with prayer.

39. Go on a prayer date instead of out to dinner or some other recreational activity.

40. Take pictures of those for whom you are praying; write prayers on the backs of their pictures.

41. Write prayer notes or letters to one another and mail them to each other.

42. Write down all the things for which you are thankful in your spouse, and then pray through that list in his or her hearing.

43. Pray together before each meal.

44. Set a time each day when you will pray with each other.

45. Ask your children to pray for the two of you together.

46. Kneel down before your mate and pray over their feet, crying out for God's mercy and guidance.

47. Pray the same way over your spouse's mind and hands.

48. Pray together for the lost. List the lost people you know and pray for their salvation, naming each one in your prayer.

49. Sit silently together listening for God's voice and sharing what He says to each of you.
50. Take a fixed interval of time—five minutes, one hour, twenty-four hours, or any interval you choose and pray continually with one another during that time.

PERSIST IN PRAYER!

JESUS PROMISES THAT when two agree together in prayer, wonderful and powerful effects will happen. "Again, I tell you that if two of you on earth agree about anything you ask for, it will be done for you by my Father in heaven. For where two or three come together in my name, there am I with them" (Matt. 18:19–20).

Praying in agreement with another person begins in marriage. A husband and wife become a tabernacle for the presence of Christ in their midst. A husband and wife praying by faith in accordance with His will can transform their lives, families, churches, and communities. God acts with wondrous power when we pray. How powerful are your prayers as a couple? Paul E. Billheimer indicates the power of prayer:

> That He [God] will do nothing in the realm of human redemption, since its inception, outside of this scheme of prayer and intercession is indicated by God's many pressing invitations to prayer in His Word. He not only invites us; He entreats; He importunes; He urges. He even begs us to exercise this privilege. One translator

174

has paraphrased Matthew 7:7 thus: "Ask, I ask you to ask; seek, I entreat you to seek; knock, I urge you to knock." Evidently He can do nothing without our prayers.[2]

I encourage you to pray together with your husband. If he still refuses to pray with you after walking through the tearing down of all the spiritual walls described in this book, then don't quit. Find another wife who will agree with you in prayer for your husband and family. Be persistent. Never give up.

One husband I had known for more than twenty years resisted the prayers of his wife. She tried to pray with him but rarely would he pray with her. She left books around and gave all kinds of suggestions about prayer. She tried nagging, cajoling, shaming, affirming, exhorting, and manipulating her husband to pray—to no avail. She asked others to pray for him. She read books on prayer. She went to prayer groups. One thing she did not do was give up. She persisted.

On Thanksgiving Day in 1989, God's presence powerfully touched her husband as he raked leaves in the back yard. Falling on his face before God with tears streaming down his face, he cried out to God and heard His voice for the first time in decades.

Over the years since that day, their marriage has been healed, their children restored, their ministry together has grown, and their prayer life together has matured. Not all is perfect, but they have seen many miracles performed by the hand of God because of praying together.

That husband was me. I thank God daily for my

praying wife, who persisted until God broke through to me.

Precious wife, don't give up. Don't give up unless you are willing to face your husband on judgment day and answer this question, "Why did you give up on me? I needed your persistent prayers even though I was unaware of my need. Why didn't you persevere?"

Believe me, dear woman of God. Eternity may well hang in the balance for your husband. There is just one, mighty, powerful thing you can do on your husband's behalf—pray! And that will be enough for a breakthrough! Judi and I are praying for you.

My God, I choose the whole lot. No point in becoming a saint by halves. I'm not afraid of suffering for Your sake; the only thing I'm afraid of is clinging to my own will. Take it, I want the whole lot, everything whatsoever that is Your will for me.

—St. Therese of Lisieux
19th Century a.d.

8

A FINAL PRAYER

ONE OF OUR favorite prayers for one another and for praying together is the Lord's prayer. That may sound too simple or traditional. So what? His prayer has profound and lasting impact, which is fresh and new every day. Pray the words of the Lord's prayer, inserting your name or that of your husband's:[1]

OUR FATHER IN HEAVEN, MAY YOUR NAME BE
HONORED IN _____'S LIFE.

Desire for your marriage partner to be honored, sanctified, made holy, set apart, and cherished through the power of honoring and fearing God. If your spouse fears and honors God, then...

▶ You will be loved.
▶ You will never be abused.
▶ You will be cherished.

❯ You will be treated with dignity and honor.
❯ You will never need to build a wall.

The King James Version reads, "Hallowed be thy name." When your spouse hallows God's name in his or her life, then your name will also be treated with honor and respect. How wives and husbands treat God is how they will treat one another. And if their treatment of God is better than their treatment of each other, then hypocrisy is their standard and hatred is the feeling they have for their own lives. "If someone says, 'I love God,' but hates another Christian, that person is a liar; for if we don't love people we can see, how can we love God, whom we have not seen? And God himself has commanded that we must love not only him but our Christian brothers and sisters, too [wives and husbands, too!]" (1 John 4:20–21, NLT).

MAY YOUR KINGDOM COME SOON IN _____'S LIFE.

Who's in control of your mate and of your marriage? When a spouse seeks first the kingdom of God, then all else in life is placed in the right order (Matt. 6:33). When Christ is on the throne of your lives and your marriage, then defensive walls do not have to be raised. Lisa Bevere confessed that she was out of control and loving it. When God is in control, we are out of control of our marriages, our children, our careers, our church, and our lives. Once the King of kings takes His rightful place on the throne of our hearts, then He directs our spiritual lives, our prayers, our thoughts, behaviors, feelings, and attitudes.

The Lord's prayer defines our priorities in marriage. His name is to be hallowed above all. Jesus confirms the first and great commandment: "You must love the Lord your God will all your heart, all your soul, and all your mind" (Matt. 22:37, NLT). Love both honors and fears God. Love surrenders control. The opposite of sin—and the walls produced by that sin—is not righteousness, for we have no righteousness of our own. Rather, the opposite of sin is surrender. In surrendering complete control to Christ, we receive His righteousness. "It is because of him [God] that you are in Christ Jesus, who has become for us wisdom from God—that is, our righteousness, holiness and redemption" (1 Cor. 1:30).

MAY YOUR WILL BE DONE IN _____'S LIFE ON EARTH, JUST AS IT IS IN HEAVEN.

God's *perfect will* for your spouse is his or her salvation in Christ Jesus. "This is good, and pleases God our Savior, who wants all men to be saved and to come to a knowledge of the truth" (1 Tim. 2:3–4). Spiritual walls will remain until both husband and wife are saved. In saving us, God changes us, making us new creations (2 Cor. 5:17).

Then He transforms us. "Therefore, I urge you, brothers, in view of God's mercy, to offer your bodies as living sacrifices, holy and pleasing to God—this is your spiritual act of worship. Do not conform any longer to the pattern of this world, but be transformed by the renewing of your mind. Then you will be able to test and approve what God's will is—his good, pleasing and perfect will" (Rom. 12:1–2).

God's *permissive will* in our lives is prescribed by the Word of God. All that He permits in the Word is permitted in our lives, and all that He prohibits is prohibited. The Word is not a legal code but a living Word ministered in our marriage by His Spirit. "He has made us competent as ministers of a new covenant—not of the letter but of the Spirit; for the letter kills, but the Spirit gives life" (2 Cor. 3:6). Husbands and wives are to hide His Word in their hearts that they might not sin against God or one another (Ps. 119:11).

God's *participatory will* invites us to go wherever He leads to become the new creations He calls us to be (2 Cor. 5:17). We fellowship in His suffering (Phil. 3:10–11). And we discover the new thing that He is doing: "For I am about to do a brand-new thing. See, I have already begun! Do you not see it? I will make a pathway through the wilderness for my people to come home. I will create rivers for them in the desert!" (Isa. 43:19, NLT).

Are you tired of the old walls, the dry seasons, and the spiritual wilderness in your marriage? Participate together with God in a new thing for your relationship. Become His ambassador of reconciliation by taking the new thing He is doing in your marriage to other married couples.

All this newness of life is from God, who brought us back to himself through what Christ did. And God has given us the task of reconciling people to him. For God was in Christ, reconciling the world to himself, no longer counting people's sin against them. This is the wonderful message he has given us to tell

others. We are Christ's ambassadors.
—2 CORINTHIANS 5:18–20, NLT

Be an ambassador for Christ with the witness of your marriage. Once Christ has shattered your spiritual walls, take His Spirit with you to other marriages so that they might be reconciled in Him.

GIVE _____ THE FOOD HE/SHE NEEDS FOR TODAY.

Daily bread for both our spiritual and physical beings cannot be old, stale stuff from yesterday or a half-baked loaf from tomorrow that isn't ready yet. His grace is sufficient to meet our needs in marriage one day at a time. We come to Him daily in prayer. He meets our needs daily. He feeds us the bread of His Word, of Himself, as the bread of life. And He provides for all our physical needs as well. It doesn't matter how bad spiritually your marriage was yesterday. Today, fresh bread is ready and available if you will simply partake. Today, fresh winds are blowing through your prayer life.

Go for all that God has for you today in your marriage. Be refreshed spiritually today regardless of what pain the past has held or what fear the future may threaten.

As a couple, remember that you have nothing to fear, nothing to lose, and nothing to hide. Go for broke in prayer today, claiming by faith all that God has for you. Know this: "You parents—if your children ask for a loaf of bread, do you give them a stone instead? Or if they ask for a fish, do you give them a snake? Of course not! If you sinful people know how to give good gifts to your children, how much more will your heavenly Father give good gifts to those who ask him" (Matt. 7:9–11, NLT).

AND FORGIVE _____, JUST AS HE/SHE HAS FORGIVEN THOSE WHO HAVE SINNED AGAINST HIM/HER.

Forgiving one another opens you up to receive forgiveness. You cannot accept your husband's forgiveness as long as you have not forgiven him. And neither of you can accept God's forgiveness as long as you grasp unforgiveness in your life.

Forgiveness is not an option. Jesus states plainly: "If you forgive those who sin against you, your heavenly Father will forgive you. But if you refuse to forgive others, your Father will not forgive your sins" (Matt. 6:14–15, NLT).

AND DON'T LET _____ YIELD TO TEMPTATION, BUT DELIVER HIM/HER FROM THE EVIL ONE.

Apply the blood of Jesus Christ in prayer for protection over your spouse, your family, your home, your church, and all your activities. Do the same with your children, friends, and pastor.

Together with your spouse, pray the blood of Christ over them. What power such a simple prayer will have!

"Just think how much more the blood of Christ will purify our hearts from deeds that lead to death so that we can worship the living God. For by the power of the eternal Spirit, Christ offered himself to God as a perfect sacrifice for our sins" (Heb. 9:14, NLT).

The blood protects us from the sin of building walls that hinder and even destroy our relationships with spouses, family, friends, and others in the church and in the world.

FOR IN _____'S LIFE YOU WILL BUILD YOUR KINGDOM AND MANIFEST YOUR GLORY FOREVER AND EVER. AMEN.

You and your husband are mighty spiritual warriors in God's kingdom. The enemy would like nothing more than to keep you prayerless through whatever wall you may build.

Help one another put on your spiritual armor. Take a moment to consider this: In ancient times the armor was much too heavy for a person to put on by himself. He needed a partner to help him become equipped for the battle.

In Ephesians 6:11, Paul writes, "Put on all of God's armor so that you will be able to stand firm against all strategies and tricks of the Devil" (NLT). Paul is not appealing for single warriors or lone rangers to stand alone against the enemy. Rather, he writes to believers as the body of Christ, the army of God, soldiers of Christ, and mighty warriors to stand together against the enemy, supporting one another. A lone sheep is an easy target for a wolf just as a solitary Christian is easy prey for the lion—the devil—who goes about seeking whom he may devour (1 Pet. 5:8).

Husbands and wives need each other's help to put on God's armor and prepare to do battle. Pray the following prayer over your spouse:

Jesus, arm _____ with the belt of truth.
Cover _____'s heart with your breastplate of righteousness.

Fit _____'s feet with the readiness of the gospel of peace.

Help _____ take up the shield of faith to extinguish the fiery darts of the evil one.

Put Your helmet of salvation on _____'s head.

Equip _____ with the sword of the Spirit which is Your Word.

Lord Jesus, You be _____'s covering and armor.

—Amen

So what is the battle? Obviously, it's not defeating the enemy. That was done at the cross where Christ destroyed the works of the devil. (See 1 John 3:8.) The battle has already been won. Satan, sin, and death have been defeated. Our battle is prayer that claims, establishes, and overcomes the enemy as he seeks to rob, kill, and destroy the abundant life we have in Christ (John 10:10). Prayer is the effective weapon that repels the attacks of the enemy. The purpose of the armor is to be equipped to pray!

Together in prayer, you and your husband—armed with God's armor—are to pray…

▶ *At all times.* That means every day.
▶ *On every occasion.* That means every situation.
▶ *In the power of the Holy Spirit.* That means you will overcome every weakness not by might, not by your own power, but by His Spirit.
▶ *With all kinds of prayer.* That means adoration, thanksgiving, confession, praise, repentance, petition, and intercession. Learn to use every type of prayer.

186

▶ *Always.* That means to persist in prayer. Pray through the attack to the victory on the other side. On the other side of your persistent prayers people are being saved, delivered, healed, and set free.

▶ *Staying alert, praying for all the saints.* We need one another. Praying for all the saints begins with praying together as husbands and wives. (See Ephesians 6:18.)

In your marriage, let God's Spirit build His kingdom in the hearts of His people through prayer and the Word. Turn away and repent of your walls now. Turn to the Lord in prayer.

> But whenever anyone turns to the Lord, then the veil [and the wall] is taken away. Now, the Lord is the Spirit, and wherever the Spirit of the Lord is, he gives freedom. And all of us have had that veil [and walls] removed so that we can be mirrors that brightly reflect the glory of the Lord. And as the Spirit of the Lord works within us, we become more and more like him and reflect his glory even more.
> —2 CORINTHIANS 3:16–18, NLT

Walls block the glory; mirrors reflect the glory of the Lord. Walls hinder prayer; mirrors reflect prayer. Walls keep us in the dark, but mirrors shine the light of Christ into our lives. Mirror Christ in the life of your spouse and not only will the walls come tumbling down, they will stay down permanently.

Here is my prayer for you:

Lord Jesus, shatter every wall in this marriage. Release Your Spirit to pray through this marriage with power. By Your Spirit, convict each spouse, exposing sin so that this couple will be driven to their knees in repentance. Clothe them with Your armor so that they might pray all the time, in all occasions, with all kinds of prayer, for all situations, interceding for all the saints so that their marriage will mirror the glory of Christ to all.

—Amen

Notes

CHAPTER 2
IF YOU AREN'T THE PRIEST OF THE FAMILY, WHO IS?

1. David Ferguson & Don McMinn, *Top 10 Intimacy Needs* (n.c., n.s.: Intimacy Press, 1994).

CHAPTER 3
BREAKING DOWN THE SPIRITUAL WALLS OF . . .
UNFULFILLED EXPECTATIONS, UNIMPLEMENTED PLANS, AND UNKEPT PROMISES

1. John Bevere, *The Bait of Satan* (Lake Mary, FL: Creation House, 1995), 24.

2. Edward M. Bounds, *The Complete Words of E. M. Bounds on Prayer* (Grand Rapids, MI: Baker Book House, 1990), 409.

CHAPTER 4
BREAKING DOWN THE SPIRITUAL WALLS OF . . .
UNMET NEEDS, UNPRIZED GIFTS, AND UNRECOGNIZED SACRIFICES

1. John Powell, *Unconditional Love* (n.c., n.s.: Argus Communications, 1978), 80.

CHAPTER 5
BREAKING DOWN THE SPIRITUAL WALLS OF . . .
UNHEALED HURTS, UNRESOLVED ANGER, AND UNREPENTED OFFENSES

1. Gary Smalley, *Making Love Last Forever,* (Dallas, TX: Word Publishing, 1996), 90–91.

2. Ibid., 17.

3. Bevere, *Bait of Satan,* 24–25.

CHAPTER 6
BREAKING DOWN THE SPIRITUAL WALLS OF . . .
UNCONFESSED SIN, UNDIGNIFIED COMMUNICATION,
AND UNFEELING RESPONSES

1. A. W. Tozer, *Five Spiritual Vows* (Harrisburg, PA: Christian Publications, n.d.).

2. Henry Cloud and John Townsend, *False Assumptions* (Grand Rapids, MI: Zondervan, 1994), 155.

3. Neil T. Anderson and Dave Park, *Busting Free* (Ventura, CA: Gospel Light, 1994), 131.

CHAPTER 7
CONFESSION: REPENTANCE THAT HEALS MARRIAGES

1. Paul [David] Yonggi Cho, *Prayer: Key to Revival* (Dallas, TX: Word Publishing, 1987), 29–30.

2. Paul E. Billheimer, *Destined for the Throne* (Fort Washington, PA: Christian Literature Crusade, 1975), 44–45.

CHAPTER 8
A FINAL PRAYER

1. Quotes from the Lord's prayer in Matthew 6 are adapted from the New Living Translation.

Appendix

PRAYING FROM THE SCRIPTURES

Praying From the Scriptures

The Scriptures are filled with principles that can lay the foundation for a vibrant prayer life for your marriage. These principles can tear down the walls that prayerlessness has built.

Are you willing to set aside how you feel for the moment and come to Christ as one in Him, asking Him to tear down your walls? You have that privilege. Will you take advantage of it?

I not only invite you, I strongly urge you to ask your husband to pray with you, using the following prayers that have been adapted from God's Word.

Pray these prayers together daily until both of you know that the walls have been destroyed by Christ. Then move on to praying blessing upon each other.

Blessing One Another

Put the name of your spouse, child, family member, or any person you choose in the blanks.

The LORD bless _____ and keep him;
    the LORD make His face shine upon _____
    and be gracious to him;
    the LORD turn his face toward _____
    and give him peace. Amen.
        —ADAPTED FROM NUMBERS 6:24–26

For Prosperity

Lord, send Your rain at the proper time from Your rich treasury in the heavens to bless all the work we do. May we lend to others, but never need to borrow from them. Lord, we will be careful to obey Your commands. According to Your word, make us the head and not the tail, and always give us the upper hand. Amen.
    —ADAPTED FROM DEUTERONOMY 28:12–14, NLT

A Blessing Upon Children

Put the name(s) of your child(ren) in the blanks.

May God, the God before whom my ancestors walked in faith, the God who has been my shepherd all my life, and the Angel who has kept me from all harm—may He bless my children. May they preserve my name and the names of my spiritual parents and grandparents.

192

And may my child(ren) _____ become a
mighty nation. Amen.

—ADAPTED FROM GENESIS 48:15–16, NLT

Thanksgiving for a Child

After Hannah was barren for years, during which
time she prayed for a child, God blessed her with the
birth of Samuel. This is her prayer of thanksgiving.

My heart rejoices in the LORD!
    Oh, how the LORD has blessed me!
Now I have an answer for my enemies,
    as I delight in your deliverance.
No one is holy like the LORD!
    There is no one besides you;
    there is no Rock like our God.

Stop acting so proud and haughty!
    Don't speak with such arrogance!
The LORD is a God who knows your deeds;
    and he will judge you for what you have
      done.
Those who were mighty are mighty no more;
    and those who were weak are now strong.
Those who were well fed are now starving;
    and those who were starving are now full.
The barren woman now has seven children;
    but the woman with many children will
      have no more.
The LORD brings both death and life;
    he brings some down to the grave but
      raises others up.
The LORD makes one poor and another rich;

he brings one down and lifts another up.
He lifts the poor from the dust—
    yes, from a pile of ashes!
He treats them like princes,
    placing them in seats of honor.

For all the earth is the LORD's
    and he has set the world in order.
He will protect his godly ones,
    but the wicked will perish in darkness.
No one will succeed by strength alone.
    Those who fight against the LORD will be
        broken.
He thunders against them from heaven;
    the LORD judges throughout the earth.
He gives mighty strength to his king;
    he increases the might of his anointed one.
                —1 SAMUEL 2:1–10, NLT

Blessing Upon Your Family

Then King David went in and sat before the Lord and prayed, "Who am I, O Sovereign Lord, and what is my family, that you have brought me this far?...What more can I say? You know what I am really like, Sovereign Lord. For the sake of your promise and according to your will, you have done all these great things and have shown them to me.

"How great you are, O Sovereign LORD! There is no one like you—there is no other God. We have never even heard of another god like you!...And now, O LORD God, do as you have promised concerning me and my

194

family. Confirm it as a promise that will last forever."

—2 Samuel 7:18, 20–22, 25, nlt

For Mercy and Forgiveness

A prayer by Solomon when the temple was dedicated.

> O Lord, God of Israel, there is no God like you in all of heaven and earth. You keep your promises and show unfailing love to all who obey you and are eager to do your will...Listen to my prayer and my request, O Lord my God. Hear the cry and the prayer that your servant is making to you. May you watch over this [household] both day and night, this place where you have said you would put your name. May you always hear the prayers I make toward this place. May you hear the humble and earnest requests from me and [my family] when we pray toward [Your face]. Yes, hear us from heaven where you live, and when you hear, forgive. Amen.

—2 Chronicles 6:14, 19–21, nlt

For God's Shepherding

Insert your spouse's name, child's name, or another person's name for whom you are interceding.

> The Lord is _____'s shepherd;
>   He has everything he needs.
> The Lord lets _____ rest in green meadows;

195

He leads him beside peaceful streams.
He renews his strength.
He guides _____ along right paths,
    bringing honor to his name.
Even when _____ walks
    through the dark valley of death,
he will not be afraid,
    for You are close beside him.
Your rod and Your staff
    protect and comfort him.
You prepare a feast for _____
    in the presence of his enemies.
You welcome _____ as a guest,
    anointing his head with oil.
    His cup overflows with blessings.
Surely Your goodness and unfailing love will
    pursue _____
    all the days of his life,
and _____ will live in the house of the LORD
    forever. Amen.
                    —ADAPTED FROM PSALM 23, NLT

For Protection

_____, who lives in the shelter of the Most High,
    will find rest in the shadow of the Almighty.
This _____ declares of the LORD:
    He alone is his refuge, his place of safety;
    The LORD is _____'s God, and he is trusting
        Him.
For He will rescue _____ from every trap
    and protect him from the fatal plague.
He will shield _____ with His wings.
    He will shelter him with His feathers.

His faithful promises are _____'s armor and
    protection.
I pray that _____ will not be afraid of the terrors
    of the night,
    nor fear the dangers of the day,
nor dread the plague that stalks in
      darkness,
    nor the disaster that strikes at midday.
Though a thousand fall at his side,
    though ten thousand are dying around
      him,
    these evils will not touch _____.
But _____ will see it with his eyes;
    _____ will see how the wicked are punished.

If _____ makes the LORD his refuge,
    if he makes the Most High his shelter,
no evil will conquer him;
    no plague will come near his dwelling.
For the LORD orders His angels
    to protect _____ wherever he goes.
They will hold him with their hands
    to keep him from striking his foot on a
    stone.
_____ will trample down lions and poisonous
    snakes;
_____ will crush fierce lions and serpents
    under his feet!

Lord, I trust Your promise: "I will rescue those
    who love me.
    I will protect those who trust in my name.
When they call on me, I will answer;
    I will be with them in trouble.

197

I will rescue them and honor them.
I will satisfy them with a long life
    and give them my salvation." Amen.
                    —Adapted from Psalm 91, nlt

For God's Gentle Correction

You might also substitute your spouse's name for "me."

I know, Lord, that a person's life is not his own. No one is able to plan his own course.
So correct me, Lord, but please be gentle. Do not correct me in anger, for I would die. Amen.
                    —Jeremiah 10:23–24, nlt

Praying Repentance

A prayer of repentance by Daniel.

O our God, hear your servant's prayer! Listen as I plead. For your own sake, Lord, smile again on your desolate [household]. O my God, listen to me and hear my request. Open your eyes and see our wretchedness. See how [our lives] lie in ruins—for everyone knows that [we are] yours. We do not ask because we deserve help, but because you are so merciful. O Lord, hear. O Lord, forgive. O Lord, listen and act! For your own sake, O my God, do not delay, for your people and your [household] bear your name. Amen.
                    —Daniel 9:17–19, nlt

Joyful Prayer

> Even though the fig trees have no blossoms, and there are no grapes on the vine; even though the olive crop fails, and the fields lie empty and barren; even though the flocks die in the fields, and the cattle barns are empty, yet I will rejoice in the Lord! I will be joyful in the God of my salvation. The Sovereign Lord is my strength! He will make me as surefooted as a deer and bring me safely over the mountains. Amen.
>
> —HABAKKUK 3:17–18, NLT

For Wisdom

A prayer by Daniel. You may wish to replace "me" with the name of your spouse.

> Praise the name of God forever and ever,
>   for he alone has all wisdom and power.
> He determines the course of world events;
>   he removes kings and sets others on the
>   throne.
> He gives wisdom to the wise
>   and knowledge to the scholars.
> He reveals deep and mysterious things
>   and knows what lies hidden in darkness,
>   though he himself is surrounded by light.
> I thank and praise you, God of my ancestors,
>   for you have given me wisdom and
>   strength. Amen.
>
> —DANIEL 2:20–23, NLT

Glorifying God

The virgin Mary, upon learning that she will give birth to the Messiah, gave praise to God by saying.

> Oh, how I praise the Lord.
>> How I rejoice in God my Savior!
> For he took notice of his lowly servant girl,
>> and now generation after generation
>>> will call me blessed.
> For he, the Mighty One, is holy,
>> and he has done great things for me.
> His mercy goes on from generation to
>>> generation,
>> to all who fear him.
> His mighty arm does tremendous things!
>> How he scatters the proud and haughty
>>> ones!
> He has taken princes from their thrones
>> and exalted the lowly.
> He has satisfied the hungry with good things
>> and sent the rich away with empty hands.
> And how he has helped [me!]
>> He has not forgotten his promise to be
>>> merciful.
> For he promised our ancestors...
>> to be merciful to them forever.
>>>> —LUKE 1:46–55, NLT

For God's Comfort

> May God our Father and the Lord Jesus Christ
> give _____ His grace and peace.

All praise to the God and Father of our Lord Jesus Christ. He is the source of every mercy and the God who comforts _____. He comforts him in all his troubles so that he can comfort others. When others are troubled, _____ will be able to give them the same comfort God has given him. You can be sure that the more _____ suffers for Christ, the more God will shower him with His comfort through Christ. Amen.

—ADAPTED FROM 2 CORINTHIANS 1:2–5, NLT

Intercession for Wisdom

I pray that _____'s heart will be flooded with light so that he can understand the wonderful future the Lord has promised to those He called. I want _____ to realize what a rich and glorious inheritance God has given to His people.

I pray that _____ will begin to understand the incredible greatness of God's power for us who believe Him. This is the same mighty power that raised Christ from the dead and seated Him in the place of honor at God's right hand in the heavenly realms. Amen.

—ADAPTED FROM EPHESIANS 1:18–19, NLT

To be Rooted in Love

When I think of the wisdom and scope of God's plan, I fall to my knees and pray to the Father, the Creator of everything in heaven and on earth. I pray that from His glorious,

201

unlimited resources He will give _____ mighty inner strength through His Holy Spirit. And I pray that Christ will be more and more at home in _____'s heart as he trusts in Him. May _____'s roots go down deep into the soil of God's marvelous love. And may he have the power to understand, as all God's people should, how wide, how long, how high, and how deep His love really is. May _____ experience the love of Christ, though it is so great he will never fully understand it. Then he will be filled with the fullness of life and power that comes from God. Now glory be to God! By His mighty power at work within _____, God is able to accomplish infinitely more than _____ would ever dare to ask or hope. May He be given glory in the church and in Christ Jesus forever and ever through endless ages. Amen.

—ADAPTED FROM EPHESIANS 3:14–21, NLT

Praise for Christ's Good Work

Every time I think of _____, I give thanks to my God. I always pray for him, and I make my requests with a heart full of joy because _____ has been my partner in spreading the Good News about Christ from the time he first heard it until now. And I am sure that God, who began the good work within _____, will continue His work until it is finally finished on that day when Christ Jesus comes back again.

It is right that I should feel as I do about _____, for he has a very special place in my heart. We have shared together the blessings of God...God knows how much I love _____ and long for him with the tender compassion of Christ Jesus. I pray that _____'s love [in our marriage] will overflow more and more, and that he will keep on growing in knowledge and understanding. For I want _____ to understand what really matters, so that he may live a pure and blameless life until Christ returns. May _____ always be filled with the fruit of salvation—those good things that are produced in his life by Jesus Christ—for this will bring much glory and praise to God. Amen.

—ADAPTED FROM PHILIPPIANS 1:3–11, NLT

Interceding for Your Spouse's Love

Spirit of God, I pray that You would gift _____ with love that is patient and kind. May his love not be jealous or boastful or proud or rude. Enable _____'s love not to demand its own way. May his love not be irritable, and may it keep no record of when he has been wronged.

Grant that _____ is never glad about injustice but rejoices whenever the truth wins out. Empower _____'s love never to give up, never to lose faith, and always to be hopeful, enduring every circumstance.

May _____'s love last forever.

When _____ was a child, he spoke and thought and reasoned as a child does. But now that _____ has grown up, give him the ability and willingness to put away childish things.

Now _____ sees things imperfectly as in a poor mirror, but then he will see everything with perfect clarity. All that he knows now is partial and incomplete, but then _____ will know everything completely, just as God knows him now.

O God, among faith, hope, and love, let love be his highest goal. Amen.

—ADAPTED FROM 1 CORINTHIANS 13:4–14:1, NLT

To Honor the Lord

I always pray for _____, and give thanks to God the Father of our Lord Jesus Christ, for I know that he trusts in Christ Jesus and loves all of God's people. I ask God to give _____ a complete understanding of what He wants to do in his life, and I ask Him to make _____ wise with spiritual wisdom. Then the way _____ lives will always honor and please the Lord, and he will continually do good, kind things for others. All the while, _____ will learn to know God better and better.

I also pray that _____ will be strengthened with God's glorious power so that he will have all the patience and endurance he needs. May _____ be filled with joy, always thanking the Father, who has enabled him to share the inheritance that belongs to God's holy people, who live in the light. For the Lord has rescued _____ from the one who rules in the kingdom of darkness, and He has brought him into the Kingdom of His dear Son. God has purchased _____'s freedom with His blood and has forgiven all his sins. Amen.

—ADAPTED FROM COLOSSIANS 1:3–4, 9–14, NLT

Direction

How I thank God for you! Because of you I have great joy in the presence of God. Night and day I pray earnestly for you, asking God to let me see you again to fill up anything that may still be missing in your faith.

And may the Lord make your love grow and overflow [toward me] and to everyone else, just as [my] love overflows toward you. As a result, Christ will make your heart strong, blameless, and holy when you stand before God our Father on that day when our Lord Jesus comes with all those who belong to him. Amen.

—1 THESSALONIANS 3:9–10, 12–13, NLT

For the Whole Person

Now may the God of peace make you holy in every way, and may your whole spirit and soul and body be kept blameless until that day when our Lord Jesus Christ comes again. God, who calls you, is faithful; he will do this. Amen.

—1 THESSALONIANS 5:23–24, NLT

For Equipping

And now, may the God of peace, who brought again from the dead our Lord Jesus, equip _____ with all he needs for doing the Lord's will. May He produce in _____, through the power of Jesus Christ, all that is pleasing to him. Jesus is the great Shepherd of the sheep by an everlasting covenant, signed with His

blood. To Him be glory forever and ever. Amen.
—ADAPTED FROM HEBREWS 13:20–21, NLT

When Suffering

I pray, Lord Jesus, that _____ will humble himself under the mighty power of God, so that in His good time God will honor him. Help _____ to give all worries and cares God, for He cares about what happens to him.

Help _____ to be careful to watch out for attacks from the devil, his great enemy who prowls around like a roaring lion, looking for some victim to devour. Strengthen _____ to take a firm stand against the devil, and let _____ be strong in faith. Let him remember that Christians all over the world are going through the same kind of suffering that he is.

In His kindness God called _____ to His eternal glory by means of Jesus Christ. After _____ has suffered a little while, the Lord will restore, support, and strengthen him, and He will place him on a firm foundation. All power is His forever and ever. Amen.
—ADAPTED FROM 1 PETER 5:6–11, NLT

Not to Fall

And now, all glory to God, who is able to keep _____ from stumbling, and who will bring him into His glorious presence innocent of sin and with great joy. All glory to Him, who alone is God our Savior, through Jesus Christ our Lord. Yes, glory, majesty, power, and authority belong

to Him, in the beginning, now, and forever-
more. Amen.

—ADAPTED FROM JUDE 24–25, NLT

For Wives

I thank You, Lord, for my virtuous and capable
wife. She is worth more than precious rubies. I
trust her, and she will greatly enriches my life.

She does not hinder me but helps me in
every aspect of my life. She takes care of my
physical needs. She manages our household
with love and diligence. She is energetic and
strong, a hard worker. She watches for bar-
gains; her lights burn late into the night.

Her hands are busy taking care of the needs
of our family. She extends a helping hand to
the poor and opens her arms to the needy.

She has no fear of winter for her household
because all of them have warm clothes. She
provides clothing for her family and dresses
with dignity and loveliness. I am proud to be
her husband in private and public places.

She is clothed with strength and dignity, and
she laughs with no fear of the future. When she
speaks, her words are wise, and kindness is the
rule when she gives instructions.

She carefully watches all that goes on in her
household and does not have to bear the
consequences of laziness. For my wife, I praise
You, O Lord. Our children stand and bless her.

Lord, with You as my witness, I proclaim:
"There are many virtuous and capable women
in the world, but _____ surpasses them all!" I

give You praise, Lord Jesus, for my wife. Reward her for all she has done. Let her deeds publicly declare her praise. Amen.

—ADAPTED FROM PROVERBS 31

For Husbands

Lord, I thank You for my husband. Help him to trust You with all his heart and not to depend on his own understanding. May he seek Your will in all that he does. Direct his plans.

His hard work and provision for his family are a blessing. Help him to fear You and turn his back on evil. Give him the desire to honor You with his wealth so that our household will be overflowing with Your abundance.

When You discipline my husband, Lord, help him not to be discouraged but to delight in Your correction. May He desire Your wisdom above wealth and fame.

Help him, Lord, to focus on good planning and insight. Give him compassion to help the needy. Guard his tongue and his heart. Keep him humble before You. May his upright life of integrity bring honor and blessing on our household. May he have eyes of love only for me. Fix _____'s heart on You. Amen.

—ADAPTED FROM PROVERBS 1–4

Select Bibliography

Boa, Ken. *Simple Prayers*. Tulsa, OK: Honor Books, 1997.

Bounds, E. M. *The Complete Works of E. M. Bounds on Prayer*. Grand Rapids, MI: Baker Books, 1990.

Copeland, Germaine. *Prayers That Avail Much*. Tulsa, OK: Harrison House, 1997.

Christenson, Evelyn. *What Happens When Women Pray*. Wheaton, IL: Victor Books, 1975.

Foster, Richard. *Prayer*. San Francisco, CA: Harper San Francisco, 1992.

Guyon, Jeanne. *Experiencing God Through Prayer*. Springdale, PA: Whitaker House Publishers, 1984.

Keefauver, Larry. *Praying With Smith Wigglesworth*. Lake Mary, FL: Creation House, 1996.

Keefauver, Larry. *Smith Wigglesworth on Prayer*. Lake Mary, FL: Creation House, 1996.

Pollock, Constance and Daniel Pollock. *The Book of Uncommon Prayer*. Dallas, TX: Word Publishing, 1996.

Underhill, Evelyn. *Abba*. Ridgefield, CT: Morehouse-Barlow, 1982.

Charisma
Book Warehouse

Yes! The same people who bring you *Charisma* magazine each month now offer you an entire warehouse of Spirit-led books! Call now to receive your FREE copy of the CBW Resource Catalog and receive 20 percent off the retail price of every title you select.

Charisma Book Warehouse is your best source for powerful, Spirit-led books by great teachers like T.D. Jakes, Joyce Meyers, John Bevere, Mike Bickle, Cathy Lechner, and many more!

The *Charisma* Book Warehouse is not a "club" that you have to join. There is absolutely no obligation to buy at any time. Simply call ***1 800 599 5750*** and start getting your favorite Spirit-led books directly through the mail for 20 percent off!

For more information on how to receive your FREE CBW Resource Catalog call

1-800-599-5750

or mail your name and address to:

CBW
P.O. Box 520670
Longwood, FL 32752-0670

Ministry Information

For other ministry materials or to inquire about speaking or leading couples' prayer seminars and retreats, please contact Dr. Larry Keefauver at:

Your Ministry Counseling Services
P. O. Box 950596
Lake Mary, FL 32795-0596
1-800-750-5306